Reboot Your Body

Nutritional secrets and lifestyle habits that can add years to your life and help avoid disease and debility.

by

Steve Shelley

I've done the research so you don't have to.

First published in 2017 as Live Healthy, Live Happy, Live Longer

A LonePenguin book
www.thelonepenguin.com

Strategic Alignment Ltd, York, England

About the author

Steve Shelley is an expert in getting to the heart of a subject and presenting it in an informative and digestible format. His interest in holistic health arose through the convergence of curiosity, personal interest and a learning opportunity. He travelled to Arizona to study with a naturopathic practice as part of the research for this book.

He has direct personal experience of how the brain can be kept alert as it grows older, having successfully completed a master's degree with distinction in his sixties. He has also been formally trained in CBT, NLP, mindfulness and coaching.

Steve's published titles include books on travel, leadership, business and wildlife. His professional experience includes working as a consultant, advisor, trainer and coach specialising in personal and organisational change and performance.

Steve is an inveterate traveller and splits his time between York and Nairobi.

For more about Steve, please see www.thelonepenguin.com.

He can be contacted on steve.shelley@thelonepenguin.com.

If you enjoyed this book, please leave a review on www.amazon.co.uk, search Reboot Your Body or Steve Shelley.

You might also enjoy Steve's book Let's Go Travel, available as an e-book on Amazon and iTunes, and as a full colour illustrated paperback on Amazon.

Introduction to this 2nd edition

It's less than a year since I uploaded the first edition of this book. Nothing has changed in the substance of what it contains but there has been some new research published which usefully adds to our knowledge and to the tips we are able to offer. The whole topic of holistic health – the intimate relationship between mind, body and environment – is slowly becoming mainstream. Almost daily in the media, new reports are highlighted which confirm both the emerging science and the growing interest in it. Today's announcement was a confirmation of a link between physical inflammation, damage to the immune system and depression. Bodily disease can cause mental disorders, and common psychological imbalances such as anxiety and depression can exacerbate physical ailments. Equally exciting is research into our 'gut biome', the colonies of bacteria which act as the interface between our foods and our health. It seems clear that our modern dependence on processed foods and our exposure to a polluted environment adversely affects our biome, thereby contributing to a wide range of serious ailments and disorders.

The good news is that many adverse conditions – both physical and mental – can be substantially avoided and ailments associated with age-related decline reversed or avoided altogether. This book tells you how.

The reference to 'rebooting' your body (and, as we shall see, your brain) alludes to computer systems which slow down and need to have their operating systems upgraded and started anew. We humans are just the same. The way we treat our bodies causes them to slow down, as demonstrated by an onset of debility and disease. But the nutritional tips and lifestyle advice provided in this book will enable you to do a full upgrade and reboot your own system.

Preface

The majority of people alive today should reasonably expect to live into their nineties. But for too many, the last 10-15 years will be at best boring, quite likely painful, and at worst so debilitating that they become a serious burden on their families and on state care. This need not be the case.

This book will show you how to maintain a healthy digestive system, build up your immune system, and adopt lifestyle habits that reduce your risk of disease, debility and decline. During the first part of our lives – the 'first third' – ill health and old age seems too far away to worry about. This is when it's all too easy to pick up bad habits that can cause trouble later. During the 'second third', we're mostly pre-occupied with family and career. So for many, it's only when retirement looms – the 'third third' of our lives – that age related ailments begin to seem all too real. It's not too late to take action then, but it is a lot more useful to adopt healthy habits much earlier.

The 'Third Third' should be the best part of your life. After all, it's probably the first time you are free to make your own choices. The sooner you learn the secrets and adopt the habits, the better it will be.

Author's note: although the book is written within a British context, it is relevant for everyone everywhere. References to the NHS (Britain's National Health Service) can be replaced by whatever government medical system exists in your country.

Ten secrets to a long and healthy life

1 - Take care of your gut (see Chapter 2)

2 - Avoid processed and sanitised foods (see Chapter 2)

3 - Cut out sugar and reduce salt (see Chapter 4)

4 - Fill your diet mostly with 'proper' foods (see Chapter 4)

5 - Boost your intake of essential supplements (see Chapter 4)

6 - Reduce stress (see Chapter 5)

7 - Manage your lifestyle factors (see Chapter 5)

8 - Cut out damaging habits (see Chapter 5)

9 - Manage your mind, re-programme your brain (see Chapter 6)

10 - Treat yourself once in a while

Contents

Live healthy, live happy, live longer

Barring pre-existing conditions and accidents, the majority of people alive today should reasonably expect to live into their nineties. But unfortunately for many, their last 10-15 years will be at best boring, quite likely painful, and at worst so debilitating that they become a serious burden on their families and on state care. This need not be the case.

When my own father died of heart failure a couple of decades ago, this was considered normal. At 78, people said he'd 'had a good innings'. Much more recently, my mother died at 92. She was able to live independently up to the end, although arthritis had put paid to her gardening and sewing, and she got around the village on an electric scooter. She was pretty cantankerous, to quote a neighbour, but I attribute that to frustration, discomfort and pain. Her longevity was, we think, due to a combination of beneficial DNA, a modestly low calorie diet and sheer bloody-mindedness. I don't mean to be flippant, 'mindset' is important, as I shall explain later. But here's the thing. If we had known ten or twenty years ago how nutrition and nutritional supplements can ward off both the infirmity we've been attributing to old age and actual disease, then my mum would not have needed the bag load of pharmaceuticals that she'd been prescribed over the years and most likely she could have been much more active. Maybe her knees, fingers and bowels would have still worked.

Ailments traditionally associated with ageing – diabetes, heart disease, immune system disorders – have been progressively striking younger people. There can be no doubt that this is due to diet and lifestyle factors such as smoking, stress and lack of exercise. But it also correlates with the domination of processed foods in our diets, with mass production and intensive farming techniques, with greater exposure to atmospheric pollutants, and with reduced exposure to natural bacteria. We shall explore these in more detail as we go. But the suggestion is that the ideal age to adopt the habits and nutrition set out in this book is in your 20s and 30s. Of course it will help everyone at all ages.

I started to study nutrition and ageing as a matter of self-interest. Now in my sixties, I should reasonably hope to have another 25-30 years ahead of me. I don't want it to pass like my mum's final years. There is a growing body of research that suggests it doesn't need to. It revolves around a holistic approach to health care and disease prevention which is typically referred to as 'alternative'. In my view it needs to become mainstream. Indeed a handful or researchers are beginning to talk about 'lifestyle medicine' in recognition of the close relationship between disease and habits beyond just nutrition.

But there is not a lot of accessible information and some of it is rather contradictory, which made me wonder what we can believe. We live in a world of 'fake truths'. As I write (Midsummer Day 2017), news reports claim this is the hottest June day for 40 years. Well, maybe it is in London, but here in York it's actually a couple of degrees cooler than it was last Monday. They're also reporting that the UK housing market is falling, but in Manchester and again here in York, demand outstrips supply. There are 'Sold' signs up everywhere. So it is with health and nutrition. You cannot always believe what you read, especially when the advice appears to shift at regular intervals. We face a mountain of dilemmas. We're told that fat is bad for you, now it's not. That artificial sweeteners are better than sugar, now they're equally bad. We're told to diet to lose weight, but it doesn't work. We try to eat less, which means we take in fewer calories, but now we're told we're becoming nutritionally deprived. For years we were advised to favour margarine over butter because it contains 'natural plant oils' instead of fat. With increasing awareness of the high degree of chemical modification made to those oils, the advice is now the exact opposite.

Health care or sick care?

Much of the problem is that the media – and the news sources that feed it – are lazy and superficial. They peddle 'sound bites' and catchy headlines. They're not held accountable for accuracy and 'truth'. Real investigative journalism is rare these days. There is also a massive prejudice in favour of conventional medicine and the pharmaceutical companies that thrive on its back. Although we optimistically call it a 'health care' system, actually it's more a matter of 'sick care'. It's designed to tackle actual ailments, not to prevent them striking in the first place.

I'm all for doctors and hospitals as places to treat injuries and serious ailments beyond our immediate personal control. But they should be a last resort, not the first place we turn to. As we shall see, even serious conditions such as obesity, diabetes, stress and depression are substantially within our own control. In fact, hospitals are not the best places to tackle such things. As an aside, I've known several people recently go into hospital with one ailment, and come out with another, or worse fail to come out at all. 'Primary health care' – preventing things going wrong – is not something that the system is good at. And it's hard to find good advice outside the system.

One thing that does seem to be true, however, is that we're on the cusp of a complete overload of that system as large numbers of so-called post-war 'baby boomers' move into their 60s and face the terrors of infirmity and dementia. Already more than 40% of 'health care' budgets are devoted to the care of this segment of society. It will only grow. But I shall argue that by taking responsibility for our own health – and maintaining it better – we can age more gracefully while simultaneously reducing the pressure on the overloaded government 'sick care' system.

Another issue I shall be writing about is food processing and the food distribution chain. The current epidemic of obesity, diabetes and dementia – which everyone seems to agree is real – correlates with a period of intensive commercial food production and mass marketing through supermarkets. We've weaned ourselves off home cooking and become addicted to mass produced junk foods. Take a look at some ingredients lists and see if you agree with me that we're being fed a diet of chemicals instead of nutrients. It's no wonder things are going wrong.

Like many people, I've suffered from the difficulty in finding reliable information and advice. For years, I thought that not needing to see a dentist meant my teeth were in good condition. What I had not learned when I was younger was that gum disease, which eventually led to the loss of several teeth, is avoidable. I've spent a lot of my life in the highland tropical climate of East Africa, but only recently have I learned that exposure to high levels of ultra violet light hastens the deterioration of the cornea, leading to early onset cataracts. It has also become common knowledge that intense UV damages the skin, sometimes leading to cancer. In my case, it caused basal cell carcinoma on my face, treatable but avoidable in hindsight.

> We're living longer, we're over-using an over-stretched NHS, we're being poisoned by processed foods and chemical additives, we can't rely on the media, and vested interests control much of the information we get.

So now I've done my own research, I've reviewed others', and I've tried a few things out for myself. What I'm presenting here is a consensus summary of best practices according to the present state of knowledge. It's a highly distilled review of what you can do to maintain your health and vitality as you get older – and to make sure you do get older. I've tried to focus on those areas where advice is consistent and is supported by research. It's not all medical, and it's not only about nutrition.

Here's the proposition

The evidence is that we have the potential, just based on current knowledge, to extend our lives by 15-20 years, to defeat the big killers of today – obesity, diabetes, chronic stress, cancer – and to reduce the threats of dementia and Alzheimer's. As well as preventing, or reducing the probability of, disease and disability, there is evidence too that a lot of serious ailments can be more effectively tackled through nutrition and lifestyle choices than by conventional medical interventions and pharmaceuticals which tend to address symptoms rather than underlying causes.

I shall also explore and explain how it's possible to 'rewire' our brains to achieve lasting change in our habits, attitudes and feelings. A third pillar is to consider our 'behaviours' – things we do – and how to modify them if necessary. People of all ages know by now that healthy eating is important even if they don't do it. They know that smoking kills, even if they do it. They know we have different needs as adults and parents than when we're growing up. But it seems that hardly anyone plans proactively for the 'third third', when the kids have left home, you've parted company with your career or employer, and now it's just you and your partner with another 30 years to kill. But you don't have to be stuck with the mindsets and habits inherited from the earlier phases of your life. Change is notoriously hard to achieve, but it can be done.

Much about this 'holistic' approach is based on natural, plant-based, sometimes traditional, remedies. While the science behind it can seem elusive, I've tried to simplify things in order to provide a practical guide. But I am writing as a lay health coach, not as a doctor. I don't have medical qualifications and I'm obliged to point out that nothing contained here constitutes medical advice. To reassure you, I'm a qualified researcher and master coach, I have an MA with distinction in the management of change, I've studied holistic medicine and Cognitive Behaviour Therapy (CBT), plus I have 30 years experience in the field. But I recommend you make your own assessments, do your own research, and come to your own informed decisions. But if just half of us could reduce our visits to the doctor by half then we could save the NHS from collapse and also save ourselves from unnecessary suffering. Win-win.

Some years ago, a surgeon told me that I was medically four years younger than my actual years. More recents tests seem to show that gap has increased to 10 years. I'm nothing special, I'm not a fitness fanatic, I'm not a fad dieter. But it seems I'm doing some things right. I hope you will feel spurred to try out some for yourself. There's no danger of getting it wrong, there are no side effects, and you can pretty soon tell what works for you and what doesn't. This 'experimental' approach is important. The evidence is that we're all significantly different in the way our bodies and brains respond to different treatments. If you've ever tried to lose weight by following someone's diet you will know what I mean. they don't all work for everyone in the same way.

What you will learn

Here is a quick summary of the key things I've learned and that I want to share with you in this book:

- a lot of disease and degeneration is avoidable – we eat, drink, breathe and live our way into it

- you are what you eat – look around you and compare people's eating habits with their body shape and appearance

- to be precise, in fact, you are what you digest – but most of us don't know whether we have problems with our gut (most of us do, or will do, to some extent)

- we all know that over-eating, over-drinking and being over-weight are bad for our health – and that dieting after the event is not a sustainable solution

- eight out of ten people who know they need to change – habits, diet, lifestyle, whatever – don't do it, even when faced with a life threatening condition

- even if we eat a 'balanced diet', as we get older we absorb fewer of the essential ingredients our bodies need, but most older people eat less anyway, causing a vicious circle of decline

- most people are deficient in a range of the important vitamins, minerals, and other elements we need to function properly

- most people are deficient in the balance of their gut flora, the essential bacteria that make our digestive systems work

- but not many of us are prepared to consume the big daily platters of kale, broccoli or lentils that could provide the amounts we need, nor even the recommended nine servings of fruit, it's just not possible

- there is a range of natural substances, mostly derived from plants, that can significantly fill the gaps and fight off age-related degeneration

- our brains and our emotional states need taking care of just as much as the rest of our bodies

- there is growing evidence that we can deliberately 're-programme' our brains to better manage our bodies and our emotions

- and there is a set of techniques we can all use to manage and maintain our mental processes and cognitive functions.

In other words, we have the potential to reboot our bodies and our brains to achieve a healthier, happier life and avoid much of the decline that too often accompanies ageing.

> Many of us have the potential to add 10-15 years to our lives and avoid much of the disease, debility and discomfort that is all too often part and parcel of people's latter years.

1 What goes wrong as we age

A lot of people find as they age that they forget things, they can't think so clearly, are often in pain, can't walk, and can't sleep through the night. For many, it's a lot worse. The evidence seems to be that most people will spend their last 10-15 years debilitated, disabled and/or depressed. In this chapter, I shall try to explain why this is, and how it can be prevented.

Throughout our lives, our bodies rebuild themselves many times over as cells reproduce and die in an unending cycle. But a number of things can go wrong which slow and may eventually halt this cycle of renewal. Cell reproduction takes energy which is supplied by specific cells called mitochondria. That energy can diminish due to inadequate nutrition or to external influences such as exposure to smoke and pollution which can damage the cells' DNA. For similar reasons, the cell copying process may throw up imperfections. We see this as blemishes and wrinkles, or experience it as aches, pains or fatigue.   Evolution favoured us to reproduce early while our bodies are in peak condition, so it's no surprise that it left things to drift a bit in later life. Furthermore, as we age, we tend to eat less, which means we're reducing our intake of essential nutrients just when we need them the most.

Wear and tear

A primary ageing factor is simple wear and tear. People who play sports in their youth often observe higher incidents of joint and muscle pain later on. This is due to mechanical damage which prevents tissue from regenerating due to direct bone-to-bone friction. If you wear out even at an ever so slightly greater rate than the body can rebuild itself, then decay and degeneration is bound to become evident at some point. For people living an apparently 'healthy' lifestyle, wear and tear of both body and mind starts to be obvious from the 50s onwards. Habits you adopted during your 20s and 30s come home to roost – positively or negatively – in your 50s and 60s and have the potential to make your 'third third' years pleasant or miserable. Bad habits like smoking or gorging on doughnuts will lead to health problems and to rapid ageing relatively quickly. But even a slight imbalance leads over time to potentially serious trouble later on. Coronary artery disease develops when the rate that fats are oxidised and deposited in the artery walls is consistently greater than the rate at which the body can remove them. Osteoporosis develops when the rate of calcium loss from bone is consistently greater than the rate at which the body can replace it. A cancer grows when its ability to multiply overruns normal limits to cell growth and the checks of the immune system.

Such problems arise when we overload or undernourish the body's natural defence mechanisms even by a small margin. Those Saturday night binges. Those days spent sunbathing. More cake than vegetables. A stressful job or relationship you can't get away from.

Much of what is set out in this book can help put some of these things right. But it works a whole lot better if you can adopt healthier habits earlier in life, and encourage others to do so. It's not so much a matter of a complete shift of lifestyle - though for many that may well be indicated - but more of what I call the power of small differences over a long time. Imagine you're driving a car in a 30mph limit, what would be the difference in distance between two cars one doing 29, the other 31? In the five minutes it takes to pass through the village, one would remain well in sight of the other, just 300 yards ahead. But multiply that by 20 years and that car would be a staggering 350,000 miles ahead. That's equivalent to the distance to the moon and half way back. It's like the effect of compound interest that at 6% over 30 years turns £100 into £574.

So, good habits versus bad habits over 20 or 30 years? Makes all the difference to the quality and duration of your 'third third'. Traditionally, we've tended to view age related degeneration as 'normal', fair wear and tear, an inevitable accumulation of damage to cells and tissues. The challenge is to slow down that wearing and enhance the repairing, so that you can continue to function into your 90s and not become dependent on 'care'. With better information and some modification to your habits, this is quite within the reach of most people.

Free radicals and oxidation

Oxidation is another cause of ageing. Although we need oxygen to live, the gas reacts chemically with many substances. Think of rust or tarnish. These are common examples of oxidation. If you cut an apple, it quickly turns brown. Bread turns brittle, meats darken and harden, fruits soften and rot. This is the result of oxidation. And it's happening to us inside and out all the time. It's why our cells need to renew. They would soon stop working otherwise.

'Free radicals' are molecules which attack the body's cells, damaging or killing them. Your own metabolism, smoking, sunbathing and strenuous exercise all produce free radicals, and the damage they do is a major cause of ageing. They contribute to the gradual deterioration of organs the chemical reaction of oxidation. Damage can be serious and widespread and lead to illnesses such as cancer, arthritis, cataracts and heart disease. Free radicals :

- exacerbate inflammation in the joints and cause rheumatoid and osteo-arthritis
- oxidise the cholesterol in our blood leading to heart disease
- attack the mitochondria (cells' power generators) and impair cells' energy balance
- damage parts of our eyes leading to cataracts and blindness
- degrade the DNA in our body cells, which can either kill them or turn them cancerous
- play a major role in gingivitis, asthma, Alzheimer's, pancreatitis and ulcerative colitis
- are implicated in most major non-infectious diseases and inflammation.

Smoking floods the body with a vast tide of free radicals, as does exposure to other kinds of environmental toxins and pollution. If the damaged cells are in the kidney, kidney function will be impaired. If the affected cells are in the skin, it will lead to a loss of tone and texture. Free radical damage is an important cause of liver disease. Anti-oxidants, including Vitamin E and flavonoids from red wine and milk thistle, have been shown to protect the liver. But hardly anyone eats a diet containing enough of all the anti-oxidant minerals, vitamins and other anti-oxidant compounds we need. This is why most of us die of free radical-related disease. Boosting anti-radical defences should improve health and life span. Anti-oxidants reduce free radical damage and they can be found in a number of foodstuffs, as we shall see later. The better your defences against free radicals, the longer you're likely to live.

Inflammation

Researchers are beginning to observe that ageing, and age-related disease, is the result of 'chronic sub-clinical inflammation', continuous and unnoticed until it causes enough damage to hurt and to show. It's 'chronic' because it's typically caused by exposure over a prolonged period of time to things like tobacco smoke, fumes and poor food choices. Conditions like anger and stress can contribute by simmering silently in the background. All this contributes to faster ageing and shorter life. We take too little exercise, we eat too many calories in the form of rich, processed foods, and we don't get enough of the vital micro-nutrients that many of these same processed foods are deficient in. And so, slowly, things go wrong. Our organs begin to fail, cells run out of control and, gradually, our health begins to suffer.

> "There is overwhelming evidence that you can slow ageing by reducing or preventing the damage caused by chronic inflammation." Dr Paul Clayton.

Inflammation is exacerbated by obesity (fat), and exposure to particulate emissions (eg diesel fumes, smoke), pesticides (including household insecticides) and free radical damage. You may not know if you're suffering from inflammation unless it shows as a chronic condition on your skin. It is considered to be a factor in almost all chronic diseases including rheumatoid arthritis, Crohn's, diabetes, depression, heart disease, stroke, Alzheimer's, some cancers, and 'age related frailty'. Chronic gum disease, gingivitis, can export 'inflammation' to other parts of the body which is why it can increase the risk of heart disease. It has also been shown as a causative factor in mental disorders such as depression. Chronic inflammation is largely due to nutritional and lifestyle imbalances which compromise the immune system. But as we shall see, there are remedies which can boost natural front line immunity and help clear infections.

Killer conditions

In earlier times, infectious diseases such as typhoid, cholera, tuberculosis, polio, diphtheria, and smallpox were major killers, particularly in childhood. These have been partially, in some cases fully, eradicated through a combination of sanitation and vaccination. Nowadays, the main causes of death in the UK are cancers (76%) and heart disease, but the latter has now been overtaken by dementia (2015) especially in women. The main reason is that people are living longer. Respiratory diseases account for 24% and infections now only 3%. The side effects of pharmaceutical drugs have become a major killer, as have infections picked up in hospitals, the very place you go to find a cure. Paradoxically, it is entirely possible that the very success in treating infectious diseases has contributed to modifying our gut flora which in turn has become a case of a wide range of adverse conditions.

By the time we get into our 60s, a staggering five out of six of us will suffer one or more of the chronic diseases: heart disease, diabetes, arthritis, cancer or osteoporosis. This is a damning indictment of our unhealthy lifestyles, and much of the blame can be laid at the door of poor nutrition which we'll look at in detail as we go. Statistics also show that more than 50% of people over 55 suffer from arthritis. It is reckoned that 50% of us will end up with some level of age related hearing loss. There is some evidence that this, and many other conditions, as we shall see, can be ameliorated by means of a calorie restricted diet plus anti-oxidants, though so far as I can tell, hearing loss is one area far less studied although regrettably common.

Chronic worries, repressed anger and depression have all been shown to impair the workings of the body's immune defences which opens the door to the whole range of potential ailments and infections, including auto-immune disorders where the immune system attacks the body itself. The reason why long term stress kills is that it not only damages the immune system but also the cardiovascular system, the digestive system and the hormonal system. The effects of stress include an increase in blood sugars and blood pressure, which in turn increases the risk of coronary artery disease. The key to ageing and age-related disease, seems to be insulin, when it's production is thrown out of kilter by too much sugar. Carbohydrates, especially starch, trigger insulin production and act as a contributory factor in heart disease, diabetes and cancer.

2 Some things you need to know

Many of us are living with less than ideal health due to the interaction of high stress levels, disrupted sleep patterns and inadequate nutrition. I think there are two main reasons. One is that we quickly adjust. We don't even know we're suffering, and we may even feel confidently 'on top of things' until the body and brain start to shut down. Secondly, there is a dearth of information 'out there'. In this chapter, I'm going to give you a quick overview of some of the most important areas we really need to know more about in order to maintain a healthy lifestyle and live to a ripe old age. The first is the gut, which is vitally important because it's the primary gateway for everything our bodies need (apart from oxygen which comes through the lungs). Then we'll look at the brain, which is supposed to be in control, but we have to wonder how well it works if it repeatedly sends out instructions to eat sugary foods or think depressing thoughts. Then there's the issue of the foods we eat and why the revolution in processing, marketing and distribution is actually contributing to disease, debilitation and premature death. Finally, there are some things you need to know about the way governments 'manage' our health and how the media reports it. But first a bit of evolutionary history to put things into perspective.

We're hunter-gatherers at heart

To understand what we eat, how we eat and what out bodies need, it's revealing to consider how we evolved as a species. Much about our lifestyles and the ailments that occur can be attributed to a mismatch between ourselves and our environment. Modern development and all that it brings has taken place in all meaningful senses only within the past few hundred years. Our bodies on the other hand are essentially several hundred thousand years old in design and function. Pretty much everything about us evolved over millennia in the forests, savannas and seashores that nurtured homo sapiens during our early existence living as bands of hunter-gatherers.

It may seem obvious, but in those formative days we didn't have the use of electricity, transport or supermarkets, things which seem indispensable now. On the other hand, we still indulge in a wide variety of activities that reflect our hunter-gatherer past and through which we try keep us in touch with the land: fishing, camping, hiking, travel, barbecues, gardening, home cooking. We're good at the survival skills associated with a hunter-gatherer life, otherwise we wouldn't be here to talk about it.

Our bodies and their supporting bacterial colonies did most of their evolutionary adjustment in those distant times which characterised our existence up to the end of the past ice age 15-30 thousand years ago. Unlike most other species, humans are omnivores. Those who could eat pretty much anything became more robust, which helped them survive extremes of season, climate and geography. Those who were content to eat whatever was available were more likely to stay in good health, breed more offspring and live longer. Those with ready access to 'good' foods obviously did better than those who struggled to find enough to eat. 'Omnivore-ism' is a very successful evolutionary survival mechanism. But the hunter-gatherer lifestyle required us to consume quite a lot more calories than we do today, in order to provide the necessary energy levels for foraging, hunting and migrating. Of course, everything in those days was 100% natural.

Settled agriculture came about more recently, around 7-10 thousand years ago. This increased the availability of foodstuffs such as grains, meats and cow's milk and their derivatives. Although the quantity of available foods increased, the range and natural quality reduced from the earlier phase of our development. There is no doubt that this domestication of plants, birds and animals aided the growth of human populations. And you might think we should have adjusted to it by now. But there is some evidence, as shown for example but an intolerance of dairy or wheat products, that our guts have still not fully adapted to this change to a domesticated diet.

Preserved and processed foods, in comparison, started to become available barely 200 years ago. And really, we've had only 50 years exposure to intensive farming, processed foods and mass distribution of the now ubiquitous refined foods with their chemical additives. Our ability as a species to eat pretty much anything – thanks to our omnivore guts – has meant that we've been able to function adequately on these new diets and continue to reproduce. Most deficiencies become apparent only as we pass breeding age. Consequently, our systems have not yet evolved further. Given a few more thousand years, particularly if people continue to delay breeding age, we may collectively develop the ability to digest these 'new' foods better. But that doesn't help us as individuals right now. We're hostages to our past. To all intents and purposes, we're still living with hunter-gatherer guts.

The gut and digestion

Until the early 20th century, about a third of all children died before reaching adulthood, from a combination of malnutrition and infectious diseases. For teens and adults, warfare and street violence could be added to the list of causes. But this figure has dropped to less than 5% with better hygiene, sanitation, nutrition and medical advances, and fewer wars involving fewer people. Other trends are less favourable. Obesity doubled across 70 countries surveyed between 1980 and 2015. More people are dying of being overweight now than from starvation. This has been accompanied by a similar rise in allergic diseases such as asthma and eczema caused by over-active immune systems. This is now thought to have been, as much as anything, the result of changes in the types and amounts of bacteria we're exposed to both in our environment and in our guts – what I've referred to already as 'gut flora'.

It's an odd thought that our bodies – actually our guts – host some 2kg of live bacteria (the 'micro-biome') which help to process the foods we eat. Without them, we would die. It's a symbiotic kind of relationship and we could speculate whether our bodies are a vehicle for bacterial survival and reproduction or whether those bacterial colonies are a convenient mechanism for aiding our digestion. The fact is we can't live without them. Weird. But it's so relevant and so important that some researchers are beginning to think of humans as an ecosystem rather than a single species of mammal. Of the total number of cells in our bodies, it is reckoned that 60% are 'non-human', ie bacteria of one sort or another, millions of them. This gut biome is implicated one way or another in virtually all the conditions mentioned in this book. and its complexity helps to explain why everyone's system is different.

Even more weird is that the gut – the intestines, colon and bowel – possesses its own brain. The phrase 'gut feel' has a basis in fact. The so-called enteric system communicates with other organs including the main brain via the vagus nerve. This means, quite literally, that our bacterial colonies transmit messages to the brain in the head telling it what they want us to do. If you think you are consciously choosing a bag of crisps ("because I'm hungry") instead of nibbling on a carrot, it may actually be your bacteria crying out for more carbs! Which, as we shall see later, gives us a clue how we can re-programme that sort of 'craving'.

Killing our own biome

Typically, we have around 50 trillion bacteria in our guts, of more than 1000 species, to process foods for us. Or not, as the case may be. So it's not quite true to say that ' we are what we eat'. Or even that we are what we digest. It's more like 'we are what our bacteria colonies decide we are'. The make up of those colonies is strongly influenced by what we eat. So if you prefer doughnuts to spinach, say, then you'll likely have a preponderance of bacteria that thrive on doughnuts, because many of the others will have died off and been excreted. And since they can communicate with your brain via the vagus nerve, they will pass out the request for more of the same. That's why it's essential to restore the balance of 'good bacteria' as a first step in a balanced nutritional programme.

'Bad foods' reduce the diversity of bacteria either by killing them directly (eg poisoned by the chemical additives in processed foods) or by providing excess nutrients that help 'bad' bacteria to thrive at the expense of others. Looking after your health and looking after your weight thus becomes a matter of taking care of your gut by taking care of your bacteria. Fast foods such as burgers, chicken nuggets, fries, and sweetened 'soft' drinks can kill off your intestinal bacteria within a few days. Bacon, sausages and salamis, often considered harmless, add weight, increase blood pressure, and reduce gut bacteria. Sugars and sweetened drinks create a craving for more. They cause blood sugar spikes and accompanying insulin spikes. Processed carbs, such as crisps, fries, pasta, rice and bread that are absorbed quickly, do much the same thing, causing a surge in blood sugar that has to be taken down by means of an insulin response. Imagine what a nutrition-less stodgy mess these foods become in your stomach compared, for example, with a mouthful of kale or fruit.

Antibiotics also decimate your bacteria. That's what they're designed to do after all. Over-consumption of antibiotics – including residual traces in some of the meat we consume – is one of the causes of the current wave of allergic and auto-immune diseases including diabetes and asthma, as well as contributing to a new generation of 'super-bugs' like MRSA. I suspect that tap water could also be a problem. Chlorine is added to tap water to kill bacteria. A commonly used standard quotes a target figure of 0.5 mg/l of free chlorine. The argument is that this is safer than potentially deadly e.coli and other coliform bacteria. But isn't it reasonable to expect that chlorine may kill some bugs in your gut too? Pesticide residues (especially metaldehyde) are sometimes found in tap water.

It seems likely that more people's guts are more intolerant than we think, particularly to gluten and lactic acid. Even at a low level, gluten can contribute to inflammation in the lining of the gut which if already damaged can lead to serious conditions. Gut disorders like coeliac disease, diverticulitis, colitis and Crohn's disease are more common than we sometimes think, and they're not always accurately diagnosed. 'Leakey gut syndrome' (LGS) is a condition that may also be surprisingly common. It leads to food allergies, low energy, joint pain, thyroid problems, auto-immune conditions, slow metabolism, bloating and headaches. It's caused by tissue damage in the digestive tract allowing undigested food, proteins, gluten and bacteria to escape directly into the blood stream where they cause immune reactions. In people taking pharmaceutical drugs, or those with existing infections, this can lead to organ failure. LGS may also affect the brain – via the enteric system – and lead to anxiety and depression. Heal the gut and you can heal the brain. The main causes of LGS appear to be the 'usual suspects' of poor diet, chronic stress, toxins and biome imbalance.

Specific foods that can damage the gut include sugar, gluten, GMOs (genetically modified organisms), and cow's milk (lactose). GMOs are dangerous because they've been deliberately modified to enable crops to fight off bugs, so they fight off yours too. Sugars feed yeasts in the gut, as well as candida and other 'bad' bacteria, which can then eat holes in the gut itself. Toxins, antibiotics, pesticides, aspirin, pollution and the chlorine and fluoride in tap water can exacerbate LGS.

Differences in the make up of our individual bacterial colonies are inevitable and may help to explain why some people respond differently to certain foods – and to diets – than do others, and why weight loss programmes seem so inconsistent in the results they achieve.

The brain and cognitive functions

The brain comes into our discussion for two reasons. Firstly, it's one of the organs that can go wrong with age. Effects can range from a frustrating but manageable memory loss, to a general decline in mental clarity and thinking ability, to the far more worrying loss of personality and bodily function that is characteristic of conditions like Alzheimer's disease. 'Dementia', by the way, is a catch all term covering the wide spectrum of cognitive decline of which Alzheimer's is one of the more extreme. These conditions seem to be due to structural changes within the brain such as reduced blood flow through clogged arteries, brain cell die off, and actual shrinkage of the entire brain. Strokes cause a malfunctioning of parts of the brain and are caused by either a blocked or burst blood vessel. Hypertension can be a contributory factor.

The second issue is that since it's the brain that - supposedly - controls everything we do, it's a good idea to keep it functioning effectively. The trouble is, the brain is surprisingly easy to fool and it makes some alarmingly 'wrong' decisions at times. Nutritional deficiencies can affect the brain as much as they do other part of our bodies. Mental disorders, ie brain malfunctions, are becoming to be seen in much the same light as bodily disorders. Let's face it, the brain is just another bodily organ like the heart or the liver. Taking care of the brain will include nutrition and some of the re-programming techniques we'll share with you in a later chapter.

One such technique is called Cognitive Behaviour Therapy (CBT) which I believe can be readily adapted for all kinds of re-programming, not just for treating medical conditions such as clinical depression, anxiety and phobias. The principles of CBT revolve around a triangular relationship between thoughts, feelings and behaviours. Each influences and is influenced by the others. The trick is to recognise that 'thoughts' are not, as we suppose, the 'real me' but simply chemical and electrical signals flashing around the brain. Once you kind of hover above your thoughts and 'see' them for what they are, you can take control of them consciously and change the way you react to them. After all, it's not thoughts themselves that upset (or delight) you, it's your reaction to them, and the feelings and behaviours that result from that reaction. You can control this. You can change your thoughts, you can change your feelings, and you can change your behaviours. Exciting stuff, considering how hard it is for most people to change anything at all. More on this later.

Much about health – and about illness – is mental, or psychiatric, rather than physical and we're really only beginning to learn just how widespread are the various conditions caused by malfunctions of the brain. Depression is the most common psychiatric illness. It's estimated that 5% of the world's population suffers from depression, and numbers are on the increase. Short term depressive states are even more common and affect as many as one in five of us. There seems to be no doubt that these mental conditions, especially in older people, are one of the main contributory factors in overloading the health system and 'care' budgets. There is regrettably little research to confirm (or deny) any relationship between nutrition and good mental health, but it does seem that patients with mental problems have responded as well, if not better, to 'nutraceutical' rather than pharmaceutical treatment. Vitamins, anti-oxidants, anti-inflammatories, Omega-3, trace metals and minerals all have a role to play in brain health, as we shall see.

Some truths about processed foods

There is increasing evidence that the incidence of heart disease is much higher in people who eat a lot of sweet and starchy foods, who don't eat much oily fish, and whose diet is low in anti-oxidant rich fruit and vegetables. Certain types of fats, excessive sugar, starch and salt are responsible for many cases of obesity, diabetes, heart disease and stroke. The massive increase in the prevalence of such diseases correlates with this shift towards eating refined and processed foods in ever greater quantities. Refining takes out the natural goodness, while food processors typically add ingredients from a long list of non-natural chemicals such as emulsifiers, sweeteners, acidity regulators, preservatives, hydrogenated oils, 'trans-fats', colourants, artificial flavourings and flavour enhancers, and many other things that we humans aren't accustomed to consuming.

The following formulation is sold as a 'super-concentrated, sugar-free, water flavouring' for kids' drinks:

- citric acid, malic acid, potassium citrate, sucralose, potassium acesulfame, glycerol ester, guar gum, pantothenic acid, potassium sorbate.

Would you knowingly give that to your child? How about this one:

- glucose syrup, salt, triphosphates, diphosphates, polyphosphates, dextrose, carrageenan, potassium chloride.

Or this:

- water, starch, milk protein, salt, lactose, stabilisers, rapeseed oil, spirit vinegar, flavouring.

These ingredients account for up to 30% of a pack of sandwich ham and sliced chicken respectively. How can it be that their ham and chicken is so unpalatable it has to contain so many additives to make us buy it? And this is 'normal' practice.

28% of a pack of sausages I've just opened consists of:

- water, fortified wheat flour, salt, herbs, white pepper, diphosphates, triphosphates, sage, nutmeg, sodium metabisulphite, sodium ascorbate, sodium citrate and ammonium carbonate.

Is it any wonder that our systems produce allergic responses, that the immune system doesn't know what's hitting it, and that our cell structures become compromised? 'Carrageenan', by the way, is derived from a type of seaweed and commonly added as a thickener even in organic foods. It's not digestible, has no nutritional value, and can trigger an immune response which causes inflammation leading, in turn, to ulceration of the gut. I'd never heard of it until I started reading ingredients lists. Would you prepare a recipe at home with such ingredients? I don't think so.

The labels of food products are even more misleading than we think. Yoghurts (for example) are promoted as '0% fat' but you have to look for the small print to learn about the added sugars. In any case, it's OK, we need the fat! Salami contains glucose syrup as its main non-meat ingredient. Many commercial foods contain enormous quantities of salt because they score more highly in taste tests. Food manufacturers employ creative label writers to work hand in hand with the people formulating the ingredients in order to fool us, the consumers. So you might see three or more different types of sweetener listed low down the list to avoid having to put the catch-all description 'sugar' at the top. There is some concern, by the way, about adverse long term effects of non-sugar sweeteners. Food processors correctly assume that most shoppers are not chemists and cannot really be bothered to figure out what they're buying. Palm oil – a common ingredient in many products – has more than 200 descriptions and derivates designed to fool those of us who may be concerned that oil palm plantations contribute to deforestation.

Even the humble tin of baked beans is barely what it 'says on the tin'. 49% of the ingredients are something other than beans. Any more and they couldn't call it 'beans'! As well as tomatoes and water, the 'minor' ingredients include sugar, spirit vinegar, modified cornflour, salt, spice extracts and herb extract.

All of these tricks may be legal, but I've been trying to understand why it happens, why food manufacturers play such games with us. I mean, there is a fair argument – isn't there? – that they are actively contributing to, if not consciously causing, the epidemic of obesity, diabetes and heart disease, with the knowledge and collusion of government. There have been some tentative moves towards the inclusion of healthier ingredients, but there is a long way to go. I think there are historical reasons.

> Please read the ingredients list in your own kitchen or on your supermarket shelves. You will be – I hope – shocked at what we're eating.

Preservation and packaging

Food preservation through packaging and refrigeration dates back only to the early 1800s. Up to that time, and for many people beyond, we ate what was seasonally available in local markets. People's diet would have varied according to the availability of different foods. Shortages could lead to nutritional deficiencies, to disease, and to famine and starvation. Thus, the advent of canning and freezing in the mid 1900s, was seen as a great step forward. Quickly, producers, manufacturers and packers got together to devise how best to process and supplement their products for purposes of preservation but also to tickle the taste buds and open the purses of their customers. But in the years immediately following the second world war, food was still in short supply and families were issued with ration books. Shopping and eating continued, for a while, to be a matter of necessity and survival rather than nutrition and enjoyment. Supermarket style mass retail distribution started in the 1950s and has only more recently grown to dominate food marketing in many parts of the world. The momentum has been all about increasing availability and choice. But it has probably gone too far and now needs a 'qualitative adjustment'. Quantity has become a different problem: we buy too much and eat too much!

Not only does packaging and labelling serve to protect and identify the product and its ingredients but it must now also act to sell it, in what has become one of the most competitive business sectors. Every aspect of the layout of a supermarket and its shelves and aisles and displays is designed to persuade you, sometimes without your conscious knowledge, to buy. And one of the greatest areas of competition for your money is in pre-cooked, pre-packaged, convenience foods.

Convenience foods

Although supermarkets put in an awful lot of research into their products, their mission is to make you buy, not to make you healthy. They work on the assumption that many people are what they call 'cash rich, time poor'. In other words, you can be persuaded to pay them to do your preparation and cooking for you. Kids grow up on pre-prepared meals, and the old idea of taking time to cook a lovely homely lunch or dinner frequently seems to have disappeared, along with a 'proper' breakfast. As we've noted above, however, processed – including pre-prepared – foods tend to be overloaded with sugars and salts, and preservatives and all sorts of other 'non-food' items. Some will try to persuade you into their 'new range' of 'healthier options' as they try to follow – or lead – fads and trends. And there is no doubt that there is a current trend towards healthier eating. But while the supermarkets may indeed offer newer healthier products such as quinoa or soy milk, once you look at the labels, especially on pre-prepared 'convenience' meals, you may note that it's more a matter of one step forward and two back.

Ready-to-cook fish dishes, for example, are likely to have been injected with flavours in a brine solution. Yet salt is as dangerous for our hearts as Omega-3 is good for us. Cook-in-the-bag fish and meats may have been pre-treated to make cheaper cuts more tender. And the jury is still out when it comes to microwave cooking. There is no doubt that the humble microwave oven is a great convenience. But some authorities consider that the very microwaves that make the oven work interfere with the chemistry of the nutrients in the foods you're cooking. I have to say, however, that not everyone agrees.

Irradiation, trace metal depletion

But there's more. We have intensive farming and growth hormones which increase production but reduce the nutritional value (and flavour) of the beef, pork and chicken we eat so much of. Lamb is better because it is still largely grass fed. Plant crops grow better, faster and more furiously because of chemical fertilisers and pesticides, and more recently genetic modification. Have you noticed that many supermarket-bought fruits and vegetables can keep for weeks? They just don't go mouldy or rotten. This is not natural but it is intentional. It's due to a combination of radiation and treatment with 'approved' gases, hormones and waxes which can extend shelf life for months or even years. Now consider the implications of this. Vegetables and fruits are at the heart of all recommended healthy diets. But the likelihood is that – for many of those sold through supermarkets – both the nutritional value and natural bacterial load has significantly reduced. Yet we cannot be sure, there are no labelling requirements regarding such things. Until better information is made public about supermarkets' sourcing and value chain processing, I prefer to shop at local green grocers and market stalls. But even here you cannot always be sure of the produce's origins. Be aware and do your homework.

Soil depletion is another problem no-one is talking about. The old idea of crop rotation was intended to give the soil a chance to revive but this doesn't happen in the same way with the mega-farms which mostly produce our foods. We're beginning to realise that organic and free range is better, and why, but it can be an expensive option. 'Organic' means no artificial fertilisers or pesticides, but it doesn't guarantee the soil has not become depleted of trace minerals.

So, even if you think you're being careful with your food choices, you still cannot tell what goes on behind the scenes. The way intensive farming works, the way the animals and poultry we eat are themselves fed, the way food ingredients are shipped back and forth around the world – and what is done to them – before they end up in packets on the supermarket shelves, all this should be seriously worrying. My view is that we're still living on the momentum of over-abundance of foods after historical shortages. But now is a good time for us as individual consumers and for responsible producers and marketers to recognise that the pendulum needs to swing back towards a balance of enjoyment and healthy nutrition. Surely our health, as individuals and as a society, is more important than corporate profit. Isn't it?

Alcohol

Like smoking, alcohol consumption is listed amongst the most common causes of a range of diseases including hypertension, stroke, depression and cancers. It's also high in calories and can contribute to obesity, diabetes and dementia. It's also a significant factor in incidents of domestic abuse, traffic accidents and violent crime. But over a number of years, we've been led to believe that in modest amounts it can be good for us. A couple of glasses of red wine is typically portrayed as a valid part of the so-called Mediterranean diet, which we'll look at later. The mood enhancing effect of alcohol, in modest amounts, is considered to be beneficial. In the UK, government limits equate to eight small drinks per week but according to research from the University of Cambridge even this may be too much. The study shows that drinking alcohol in any amount is associated with a higher risk of stroke, aneurysm, heart failure and death. Drinking even one alcoholic drink on a daily basis could shorten your life expectancy, the study suggests. However, somewhat contrarily, higher levels of alcohol were linked to a lower risk of heart attack, or 'myocardial infarction'. Nevertheless, the risks seem clear.

A government health warning

The study mentioned above was released under the headline I've quoted: 'Drinking one alcoholic drink on a daily basis could shorten your life expectancy'. What does this really mean? While not wishing to diminish the value of the research, nor of the dangers of alcohol, this might be a good time to issue a warning about governments, statistics and the way they claim to manage our health. I don't want to labour the issue of statistics, but it easy to be misled. Here is the next level of detail from the alcohol research:

'Compared to drinking under 100 grams of alcohol per week, drinking 100 to 200 grams was estimated to shorten the life span of a 40-year-old by six months. Drinking 200 to 350 grams per week was estimated to reduce life span by one to two years and drinking more than 350 grams per week by four to five years.'

This could be extrapolated to imply that one drink reduces your lifespan by six weeks. Which reminds me of another study which claimed that drinking a cup of coffee could extend your life by three minutes. But look at the margin of error, it's 100% or more. The research, which I've looked at, is impeccable. The reporting is not. This is done for the benefit of the lazy journalists I've mentioned already. But it's not true. Statistics apply on a macro scale, not to individuals who, in any case, vary markedly. Some people will suffer more, some less. What they're trying to say is that overall, on balance, the population as a whole might show these kind of indicators, given enough time and participants to measure them. But this kind of qualified commentary doesn't make for the kind of snappy sound bites needed by news reporters for the top of the hour.

Unfortunately, the government manages our health precisely according to such statistics. So, for example if a particular drug is shown in trials to have a probability of reducing an ailment by, say, 60%, then it may be favoured for prescribing to everyone who calls in to see their doctor. In spite of the fact that it is known that 40% of the population will not benefit. In which category are you? You don't know. But it gets worse. Let's say for the sake of argument that another drug or treatment is claimed as reducing mortality by 50%. Does that mean we all are only half as likely to suffer? No. Because it depends on the risk factor of the disease to start with. And on our own propensity for being one of the likely sufferers. These statistics tell us very little of immediate value to ourselves. But what they do do is show how government health spending can be targeted or reduced.

So, please be cautious about what you hear in the news or read in the headlines, and delve deeper before you worry or act. These reports are nearly always available on the internet, so just download them and come to your own conclusions.

3 Holistic health: mind, body and environment

Health is not just a matter of the body. It's not just a matter of good nutrition. Our brains and thought patterns are also important. There are at least three elements that can affect our immune system: nutrition, our psychological and emotional well-being, and, unexpectedly, the environment we live in. This includes both the socio-economic group you happen to be part of and, somewhat related, your exposure to – for example – traffic, pollution, hygienic conditions, and sources of stress. The importance of environmental factors has been rather overlooked. It is intriguingly illustrated in the aftermath of natural (and man-made) disasters, where it has been learned that people may be affected not just physically and psychologically but also in terms of their relationships and cognitive abilities.

Conventional 'health care' looks at physical symptoms and prescribes pharmaceutical 'solutions'. But these drugs are known not to work in every case, and to have side effects that need to be counter-balanced by additional prescriptions. Drugs are the typical default response to psychological problems as well. 'Holistic medicine' on the other hand looks for underlying causes of illness and these can be very diverse. 'Naturopathic' practitioners prefer more natural solutions and natural, plant-based, even traditional, remedies. Health solutions based on nutrition and nutritional supplements are sometimes referred to as 'nutraceutical'. Such approaches are unlikely to do more damage or lead to unwanted side effects. Holistic approaches like this are sometimes referred to as 'integrative health care'. The opening statement in the naturopathic practitioners' oath reads 'First do no harm', in recognition that conventional pharmaceutically-based medical practices very often do harm their patients.

Let me share a few examples to show how deep some causative issues may be. Let's take diabetes. One of the primary causes is a high carbohydrate diet, but why do people eat sweet and starchy foods? It may be a matter of convenience, of advertising, or of peer pressure. It can be due to habits gained in childhood. You could argue it might be caused by food processors, through the way foodstuffs are marketed. It could even be due to ignorance. The point is that conventional medical treatments based on insulin do not in any way tackle these multiple root causes of what is not just a personal problem but a national epidemic.

Dementia is another major concern and its causes seem to include a wide range of lifestyle risk factors. Although mostly evident in later years, the brain changes associated with dementia usually start much earlier and could therefore be avoided — to some extent, at least — by taking action before mid-life. According to recent studies, risk factors include hearing loss, educational levels, smoking, depression, physical inactivity, social isolation and hypertension.

Depression, anxiety and stress are commonplace and are also substantially due to lifestyle factors including relationships, or jobs (or the lack of them), rather than having medical causes. These conditions frequently lead to immune system disorders, heart disease or even cancer. But conventional medical approaches are unlikely to offer a viable long term solution.

A family history of smoking is known to contribute to people's likelihood of taking up the habit, even when they know how dangerous it is. Passive exposure to tobacco smoke can also lead to immune system disorders. The ban on smoking in public places is, at least, one non-medical intervention which is likely to have positive results.

> Holistic medicine aims to stop things going wrong in the first place by addressing underlying causes rather than tackling symptoms with drugs. The goal is to maintain wellness, not to treat illness.

Take responsibility

Looking at the big picture, everywhere I go I see people suffering from obesity, depression, anxiety, stress, and all the horrible diseases that arise as a result. Government-run health care systems are becoming overwhelmed and families are torn apart. While politicians argue about the need for funding, the fact is that keeping our populations alive, let alone healthy, is beyond the ability of national institutions to deliver. It takes weeks to get a basic appointment, months or years to get treatment for serious ailments. The simplest of solutions for Britain's NHS would be to reduce the number of people needing its services by 50% or more. That's not an impossible dream, if people would take more responsibility for their own health, diet and habits. But, so far as I am aware, it isn't on anyone's political agenda. For now, all the momentum is driven by food processors, pharmaceutical manufacturers and by the sheer inertia in trying to shift the way the NHS works. Politically, it is considered career suicide to contemplate tinkering with the beloved NHS.

In the UK, naturopathic medicine is considered a fringe activity. Many of those people who are qualified end up working as nutritional advisors. Conventional doctors receive very little training in it. And there's very little research being funded, for the simple reason that there are few patentable outcomes likely to give a return on the investment. You can't copyright broccoli.

At the personal level, taking responsibility for your own health demands a two pronged approach. First it means avoiding or reducing exposure to risk factors. Then it means adopting more healthy habits. These are not easy to achieve but in the next chapters, we will provide some guidance. It's more than just eating right and doing a bit of exercise. In summary, avoidance factors include smoking, sugar and starchy carbohydrates, toxic exposure, and stressful relationships and situations. What you need to get right includes nutrition, posture, mental acuity, sleep, relationships, and interests and activities.

I learned about holistic medicine and integrative health care from an experienced practitioner in Arizona. My primary motivation was simple: as I've grown older, every additional year becomes more valuable and it seems worth investing some time and effort to put off the inevitable. But the experience gave me a rude awakening. I've rarely needed to visit a doctor throughout my adult life and thought I was healthy and not personally in need attention. Wrong! Without any formal examination, my teacher was instantly able to diagnose more than a dozen ailments I appeared to be suffering from. It seems we learn to live with disease and discomfort as if it's normal.

Our brains are hard-wired to force us to act to stay alive in almost every conceivable situation. It's a deep and fundamental human characteristic which is very hard to de-programme. Evolution would not have achieved this if it simultaneously allowed our bodies degenerate. Our bodies must therefore have the capability to stay alive.

The solution sounds simple: reduce or eliminate the causes of inflammation and degeneration, and boost those habits which keep brain and body refreshed. This means, for example, staying active, curious, involved and stimulated, while avoiding stress. It also means reversing any decline in the immune system through a 'good' nutritional programme which avoids depletion of essential vitamins and minerals. The evidence is that the 20% of people aged 60 and over who don't have heart disease, arthritis, cancer, diabetes or osteoporosis are those who consume a lot more vitamins and minerals. In a later chapter, we'll look more specifically at what this implies.

Let me emphasise, this is not an 'alternative' approach. It should be everyone's primary focus and habit. 'Conventional' medicine should be the back-up for when things go wrong.

Environmental considerations

The environment impinges upon our health in very many ways. It's the third pillar along with mind and body. We continually exchange influences – both physical and mental – with the environment. This includes our exposure to bacteria and atmospheric pollutants, and our interactions with people, communities and society at large. But it goes much further. Large scale food production needs land and there are parts of the world where vast natural areas have been turned over to cattle ranching, grain crop production and horticulture. Plantations of, for example, tea, coffee and oil palms have necessitated the destruction of huge swathes of indigenous rain forest in South America, Africa and Asia. Large mono-culture farms engage in a never ending battle against their own predators: insects and disease bearing pathogens. It seems likely that the measures taken to protect crops – insecticides and genetic modification – have contributed to a major loss in populations of bees, butterflies and songbirds. As we overfeed ourselves, we're killing off our own environment and its biodiversity.

Packaging manufacturing and the distribution of foodstuffs contribute to carbon emissions which affect the atmosphere and the climate. The vast majority of packaging is these days composed of plastics which, we have come to learn, is having a devastating impact, particularly on the marine environment. It's a fallacy to think that it's OK because waste is recycled. Relatively little is recycled and plastics in particular presents challenges in waste processing due to the multiplicity of types involved. One small pack of berries, for example, may be made up of three of four types of plastic. You know how quickly your rubbish bin fills up, it's primarily due to packaging. This waste and its disposal represents a major side effect of modern mass food production and distribution. We should be smart enough to do it better, without destroying the planet and its oceans.

Enough about this, I think we've made the point. Environmental health is a reflection of our own health. Now it's time to get to grips with the specifics of what we need to do.

4 Age and disease defying nutrition

There's a good reason why the longest chapter of this book is about nutrition. Everything we think, feel or do depends on a functional body and functioning brain. Everything. Apart from oxygen taken in through the lungs, everything else goes in through the gut. Whatever we eat or drink is processed and filtered by the gut. In turn, the gut feeds all of our other organs. It's tough and resilient, but it can go wrong. And it can only process what it's fed. This is why nutrition is so vital. And why brain health and body health depends on gut health. Nutrition is not the entire story but it is the main thing. Add in physical and mental exercise, throw in a good sleep pattern, and you're pretty much made.

There is a growing awareness that the alarming epidemics of obesity, diabetes and dementia, if not solely caused by what we eat, can at least be ameliorated by eating the right kinds of foods. And there is growing evidence that this works too for many other debilitating and life threatening ailments. Most people seem not to think much about what they eat other than to stick with what they think they like and what's convenient. Both as kids and as adults, we mostly go with the flow, influenced by parents, friends, TV and what we see on supermarket shelves. This is literally killing us. It's time to wise up and set yourself up for a long and healthy later life, and most especially a pain free and disease free old age. Over-processed foods, convenience foods, depleted soils, prolonged food storage and inappropriate cooking techniques mean that the vast majority of us do not get enough of a whole range of micro-nutrients. We are suffering from 'nutrient depletion' – literally starving in a surfeit of over-processed foods.

We have become the victims of our own affluence, and the comforts that we depend on are the very things that make us ill. Our existential threats are no longer war, famine and plague, but cigarettes, burgers and chips, and motor vehicles. Compared with hunter-gatherer times, we consume half as many calories, but eat a lot more fat, a lot less protein, and hardly any unrefined carbs. All these have been replaced by refined carbs which our ancestors didn't have and didn't need.

The suggestion is that an optimal nutritional mix might add 15-20 years to our life span. Whether that's true or not, I'm ready to believe that healthy eating – and not of the boring dieting kind – will help us live healthier for longer, and avoid that horrible slow decline that afflicts many of us in our 80s and 90s. There is also no harm in trying it. There are no side effects from a good diet.

In this chapter, I'm going to set out everything I've learned about healthy nutrition. We'll be looking at what a balanced healthy diet looks like, we'll flag those 'foods' to avoid, and we'll share with you the best current advice regarding supplemental ingredients that most of us are missing. We shall also set out what I've discovered about nutritional approaches to many common ailments and age-related disorders.

Bear in mind that even if you think you are healthy, and even if you already eat well, you may still have conditions, perhaps unnoticed, that can be improved. Our immune systems need over 20 different micro-nutrients to function properly. All of us, for various reasons, are deficient in some areas and we face some real dilemmas. For example, trying to maintain a low calorie diet to control weight means we're missing out on some essential nutrients, and hardly anyone succeeds in consuming the recommended nine daily portions of fruit.

> Multiple micro-nutrient depletion due to inadequate diet may well be the ultimate cause of ill-health and premature death in the west.

None of what I am setting out here constitutes a 'fad' diet. It's based on a wide range of published opinion and practical experience, as well as on a range of supportive research. There seems to be a tendency for researchers to denigrate others' recommendations. Michel Montignac promotes low glycemic index foods. Michael Mosely recommends his 5:2 fasting diet. Then along comes Michael Greger suggesting these are wrong or irrelevant and promoting plant-based diets. I have come to realise that there is merit in most serious researchers' recommendations. But none is fully 'right' nor completely 'wrong'. We can usefully apply common sense and learn from all of them.

Then there's the issue of shopping. I have found it hard to find some of the recommended healthy products in supermarkets, and you can never be really sure where even 'fresh' foods have come from and what treatments they may have undergone on the way. Eating well and shopping well is a mission!

Let's turn now to what we really need.

Essential daily needs

In general, essential daily needs for everyone include carbohydrates, protein, fat, vitamins and minerals. Carbs provide energy, protein maintains body structure, fats feed the brain and nervous system, and vitamins and minerals ensure that bodily functions operate properly. More specifically, nutritionists advise that a healthy anti-ageing diet needs to include the following.

Pro-biotics which help balance or repopulate the gut biome. These come most usefully from fermented foods such as live full fat yoghurt, kefir, sourdough, chocolate, cheese, red wine, sauerkraut and kimchi. It is recommended to avoid commercial brands because they are no better than natural alternatives and may, in any case, have been deactivated by pasteurising.

Pre-biotics include fibre which aids digestion and helps feed our 'good bacteria'. These include inulin which comes from onions, leeks, garlic, chicory, artichokes, asparagus, and bananas and is known to promote gut and bowel function, and beta-glucans which is contained in barley, oats, flax seeds which also helps to control cholesterol levels.

Anti-oxidants encourage your body to burn fat and support anti-inflammation, anti-infection and anti-allergies. Good examples are thyme, ginger, garlic, ginseng, liquorice, chilli, ginkgo, paprika, cocoa, red wine, green tea and turmeric. 'Flavanoids' are also good anti-oxidants. These include blueberries, cherries, blackberries (especially wild picked), plums, grapes, tomatoes, parsley, apples, cocoa, peanuts, red cabbage, and aubergine. The skins of fruits have a particularly high concentration.

Carotenoids including beta-carotene, are, amongst other things, a good source of Vitamin A. They can be found in carrots, tomatoes, peppers, squash, spinach, kale, broccoli, sweet potato (the red ones), eggs, peach, apricots, bananas, and melons. Lycopene is a powerful anti-oxidant that comes from tomatoes. Lutein comes from spinach and kale and promotes eye function.

Leafy greens contain a lot of the minerals we need such as potassium, magnesium and manganese, as well a vital additives like Vitamin K, folate and betaine. Fresh spinach, kale and chard are some of the best.

Omega-3 (poly unsaturated fatty acid, PUFA) is known to support brain function and many other body functions as well as reducing the risk of heart attack, anxiety, depression and arthritis. It comes mainly from seafood, especially oily fish, but is also available from chia and flax seeds.

Vitamin C is well known to provide multiple benefits to the immune system. It builds collagen in our joints and our guts. We need quite a lot of it and the following foods are the best sources: yellow pepper, papaya, guava, orange, grapefruit, kiwi fruit, strawberries.

Vitamin E is a powerful anti-oxidant which helps protect the immune system and the skin and may help correct hormonal imbalances. It helps reduce the risk of bronchial infections and cancer. It comes from avocado, almonds, hazelnuts, peanuts, pine nuts, sunflower, pumpkin and sesame seeds, chard, spinach, kale, broccoli, olive oil, papaya and olives.

Vitamin B12 is vital to prevent neurological decline, chronic fatigue, depression and stress. Lower levels of B12 are associated with the brain shrinkage that accompanies dementia and Alzheimer's. It comes only from animal foods (veggies beware!) such as seafood (especially clams), meat, poultry, milk and eggs. Liver is one of the best sources.

Trace elements are needed in tiny amounts to act as building blocks and as catalysts for certain bodily processes. These include calcium, magnesium, potassium, copper, manganese, chromium, selenium, zinc and silicon.

Other important vitamins

Vitamin A for healthy skin, neurological function, bones and vision. Vitamin A comes from beef liver, carrots, sweet potato, kale, spinach, broccoli and apricots.

Folic acid (folate, a B vitamin) helps produce and maintain new cells, and prevent changes to DNA that may lead to cancer. It's available from a wide range of foods including greens, asparagus, broccoli, avocado, okra, seeds and nuts, citrus fruits, beans, peas and lentils.

Vitamin K promotes bone metabolism and regulates blood clotting. It comes from leafy greens, spring onions, Brussels sprouts, cabbage, broccoli, prunes, cucumbers and basil.

Vitamin D is becoming recognised as important for bone growth and to avoid osteoporosis. Our bodies produce it from sunlight but it is recommended as a supplement especially in winter. Vitamin D is less readily available from foods but does occur in oily fish. Low vitamin D levels correlate with cognitive decline, diabetes, osteoporosis and various auto-immune conditions.

Our intake of many of these essential dietary components has declined significantly and has been more than made up by consumption of processed foods, especially carbohydrates containing sugars and starches.

Healthy nutrition

The common components of food intake in societies with low incidence of cancer, heart attack and stroke are similar to the basis of the so-called Mediterranean diet which typically contains oily nuts, oily fish, olive oil, eggs, dark chocolate, red wine and garlic. To this we must add fruit and vegetables, pulses, beans and chick peas, fibre and soy products. A habitual diet based on these ingredients has been shown to reduce the risk of heart disease, type 2 diabetes, breast cancer and Alzheimer's.

Such a diet is low in processed foods and sugars. What's so bad about sugars? They're empty calories. They rot your teeth, spike your blood glucose levels, make you hungrier, and increase the likelihood of obesity and accompanying risks of disease and early death. Furthermore, coupled with fat in the shape of cake and ice cream, they're addictive.

A 'good' diet is not just a matter of low carbs or low calories, but of trying to maintain a low Glycemic Index (GI).

Glycemic Index

GI is a ranking of carbohydrate foods according to how they affect blood glucose levels. Carbohydrates with a low GI value (55 or less) are more slowly digested, absorbed and metabolised and cause a lower and slower rise in blood glucose and, therefore usually, insulin response.

You might come across the related term Glycemic Load, which is the GI multiplied by the quantity of food. There is a link where you can find the GIs of various foods in Chapter 7.

Recommended foods

A good diet that becomes a habit is one you stick to for at least 70% of the time. It should contain a lot of the following foods.

Healthy foods

- Oily fish: 2-3x a week, sardines, mackerel, anchovies, salmon (wild), tuna, trout
- Eggs: 3x a week (free range)
- Vegetables: all good but especially red peppers, carrots, beetroot, leeks, onions, artichokes, asparagus, celery, okra, fennel, chicory, sweet potato, pumpkin, butternut
- Leafy greens: especially spinach, kale, chard, rocket (ruccola), bok choy
- Cruciferous vegetables: broccoli, cauliflower, Brussel's sprouts
- Beans: regularly
- Pulses (lentils, peas): regularly, including hummus
- Grains: oats, barley, quinoa

- Fruits: aim for 9x a day — fruit is better than juice in terms of sugars — all good but especially avocado, tomato, apples, pears, pineapple, kiwi, plums, prunes, mango
- Berries: all good but especially strawberries, blueberries and blackberries
- Nuts: 2 handfuls a day (especially walnuts)
- Soy products, eg tofu
- Sauerkraut, kimchi
- Bread and baking flour: whole grain or sourdough
- Herbs, especially but not restricted to: thyme, rosemary, basil, in larger quantities than you're used to
- Spices: turmeric, ginger, cumin
- Olive oil
- Rapeseed oil
- Coconut oil
- Seaweed
- Green tea, black tea
- Coffee
- Cocoa
- Dark chocolate
- Red wine: 2 small glasses a day for up to 5 days a week (but see earlier more recent advice about alcohol)
- Yoghurt, live full fat
- Goat or sheep's milk (camel if you can find it) gives less exposure to lactose than cow's milk

What about meat? You don't need much, and the advice is still that saturated fat from red meat contributes to the risk of heart disease. On the other hand, meat is a good source of protein, iron and vitamin B12 (especially from liver and kidneys). There seems no reason to avoid meat fully, especially poultry, but red meats could be kept to 2-3 times a week. But a serious consideration is the source and quality of your meat. You probably cannot tell what feedstuffs were crammed into the cattle, pigs or chickens you buy, or under what conditions they have been reared. Sheep — mutton, lamb — is more likely to have fed naturally outdoors on grass. Remember that processed and prepared meats like burgers, sausages and ready meals contain enormous levels of fat and salt and often sugar too. But remember too, there is always the opportunity for an occasional treat.

Plant based diets

We should also discuss the growing popularity of plant-based diets favoured by vegetarians and vegans. According to some estimates, some 25% of restaurants' menu items are now vegetarian or vegan options. If restaurateurs do not offer such dishes, they stand to miss out on a rapidly growing segment of customers. It seems that many of these 'v-types' exercise their preferences not solely for health reasons but on ethical or philosophical grounds. Be that as it may, there is a powerful movement claiming provable benefits of a plant-based diet which excludes all animal products including eggs and dairy. The extreme claims made by some proponents need to be treated with as much caution as do other 'evangelistic' assertions. Relevant research is thin on the ground and frequently misrepresented. My own observations and conclusions are that v-ism does not suit everyone equally, and that it risks missing some key elements such as vitamin B12 which comes only from meat. Remember that according to hunter-gatherer evolutionary theory, humans are omnivore, not herbivores. I would however agree that it is better to emphasise plant-based foods in your diet and cut right back on animal derived products.

One well known researcher-author bans even oily fish and olive oil and provides a recommended daily list totalling nearly 2kg of vegetables and fruit dishes. Impossible. I've provided the link later however because his website has some good resources.

Health promoting, disease preventing 'superfoods'

Apple cider vinegar: claimed to have many valuable uses, helps digestion and detoxification, and acts as a natural anti-biotic, reduces cholesterol, reduces blood sugar spikes caused by other foods, taken with honey to alleviate arthritic inflammation and pain.

Bone broth: home-made chicken, beef or fish soups boost the immune system, actively promote joint health and bone strength, strengthen the gut, keep the skin firm and helps detoxify the liver.

Chia seeds, flax seeds: very good source of plant based Omega-3, fibre, protein, Vitamin B1 and essential trace elements. Gluten-free, high anti-oxidant, and help protect the lining of the gut.

Coconut oil: contains healthy natural fatty acids which are anti-bacterial and anti-fungal, helps to balance good and bad cholesterol, and doesn't burn at high cooking temperatures.

Garlic: kills bad microbes, but only in its raw state.

Nuts: packed with protein, unsaturated fats, fibre, Omega-3 and Vitamin E.

Oats: a very good pre-biotic containing beta-glucans fibre and a host of essential trace elements. Reduce risks of hyper-tension and heart disease, helpful in controlling diabetes.

Okra is one of the most nutrient rich vegetables offering vitamins and minerals while cleansing the digestive tract of toxic build-up.

Quinoa: gluten-free, high in protein, contains all nine essential amino acids, high in fibre, anti-oxidants and trace elements.

Super-fruits such as pineapple, mango, kiwi, fig, prunes, strawberries and blueberries contain high levels of vitamin C. They boost the immune system, aid the digestion, promote bone and oral health and can prevent some forms of cancer.

Soy products: good source of fibre, amino acids, Omega-3 and B vitamins, and one of the best non-animal sources of protein. Helps relieve certain menopausal symptoms.

Tepache, kombucha, miso: fermented products such as these (fermented pineapple, tea and soy beans respectively) are considered traditionally to promote health and longevity in their original communities (Mexico, China, Japan). Somewhat specialist, but tasty and worth trying. Miso powder can be used as an alternative to salt as a flavour enhancer.

Thyme, oregano, basil: natural anti-bacterial and anti-fungal properties, mood enhancing.

Turmeric, ginger, cumin: powerful anti-oxidants and anti-inflammatory, inhibit bad bacteria, boost the immune system, considered to have strong anti-cancer effects.

> Many of these food recommendations are aligned with traditional 'old wives tales': eat your greens, an apple a day, chicken soup when you're ill, chew garlic to prevent infections, eating carrots helps you see in the dark, spinach makes you strong.

Eliminate, avoid, reduce

It's one thing to fill your weekly menus with healthy foods, but the other side of the equation is equally important: what to avoid or at least cut down on. If there is still some level of disagreement regarding the disease reducing effects of foods, there is a strong consensus on those that cause problems. Most of the items on the list below are known to correlate with higher incidences of heart disease and diabetes, and possibly worse.

- Sugars, including glucose, fructose and other -'oses'.
- Refined starchy carbohydrates (eg white flour and things made from it).
- Processed foods, especially those with lots of chemical additives.
- White bread, nothing useful in it.
- Sweeteners, all of them. The body doesn't need sweeteners.
- Sodium salt: most processed foods are over-loaded with salt.
- Anything with corn syrup in it: ultra-high calories with no real benefit.
- Margarine: contains hydrogenated fats which are unhealthy.
- Plant oils (eg palm, corn, sunflower, etc) can give us too much Omega-6.
- Animal fat (lard) and anything cooked in it.

- Fried foods: risk of heart disease and cancer.
- Genetically modified foods: may contain pesticides in their DNA which could damage your gut biome.
- Intensively farmed beef, pork and poultry.
- Dairy, especially cow's milk.
- Crisps: simply unnecessary, too much salt, no real nutrients.
- White rice and pasta: processed carbohydrates considered to be risky.
- Sweetened drinks: give you a sugar kick and mess up your insulin responses, even one a day significantly increases the chance of obesity.
- Shop bought sweet desserts: as above.
- Gluten: even low levels may irritate the gut.
- Antibiotics: kill off your gut biome.

Supplements and why we need them

Almost no-one is getting the amount of nutrients, vitamins, minerals and trace elements we need for fully balanced health, disease prevention and graceful ageing. It turns out that the Recommended Daily Allowances (RDA) mentioned on food labels have little or no medical or scientific basis, and all writers on this subject recommend significantly greater amounts. For example, the RDA for Vitamin C is 800mg. Advice for fruit portions has been five a day. But evidence seems clear now that we need nine portions a day, and more like 2,000 mg of Vitamin C.

The RDA for Vitamin E is 10mg, while the recommended intake is more than ten times as much. It's a similar story for the B vitamins. Two things are clear. One is that the RDAs are meaningless. The other is that we cannot get all we need from diet alone. People over 50 especially seem to reduce their absorption of vitamins and other nutrients from food sources. As people get older, they tend to eat less anyway. Remember that phrase 'micro-nutrient deficiency', it's what's causing much of today's suffering from age related disease including dementia, heart attacks, osteoporosis, diabetes and cancer. So we need supplements.

Charts showing the main supplements we need, and a consensus on the recommended amounts, are provided at the end of the book.

Although many of these foods and supplements are promoted as having beneficial effects on a wide range of diseases and conditions, their effect rather depends on your pre-existing risk factors. So, for example, if you are already eating a balanced nutritional diet, exercising adequately, and don't have a family history of heart disease or cancer, then the benefits may be minimal. On the other hand, if you are deficient in any area, then your risks can be reduced. No-one can say for sure that you won't get any given disease. It's a matter of controlling the probability.

Currently, many commercial multi-vitamins do not contain adequate amounts of supplements. Check the labels.

Naturopathic remedies

Here are some of the conditions and diseases that can be addressed through a nutraceutical approach.

Diabetes, obesity

- Avoid sugars and starchy carbs
- Keep weight and Body Mass Index (BMI) down by following the Mediterranean, a 5:2, or low GI diet
- Eat protein with a carbohydrate
- Graze don't gorge: regular small meals
- Plenty of fibre: oats, chia
- Cinnamon as an anti-oxidant and anti-inflammatory
- Supplement chromium

Arthritis, bone mass, osteoporosis, and risk of fractures

- Vitamins C and D, Calcium, Magnesium, collagen, protein
- Anti-inflammatories
- Glucosamine with Omega-3 is used to reduce joint pain
- Vitamins B6 and B12 are recommended for arthritis
- Red onions, garlic, eggs, olives, plenty of turmeric

- Weight bearing exercise, eg 3 walks a week
- Posture and stance alignment

Hypertension

- Cut back on sodium (salt)
- Reduce meat and fat and boost vegetables in the diet
- Vitamin B3 (niacin), Vitamin D, Omega-3
- Beware statins, treat conventional dietary advice with scepticism
- Stick to a low GI diet
- Reduce stress

Memory loss and cognitive decline

- Folic acid and vitamin B12
- Greens, beans, lentils, nuts, seeds
- Eggs, fish, especially oily fish for Omega-3 and B12
- Anti-oxidant fruits, berries, vegetables and spices
- Tea, red wine in moderation
- Supplement magnesium, ginkgo

Skin cancers, cataracts

- Both conditions are exacerbated by UV exposure but can be ameliorated by anti-inflammatories and anti-oxidants
- Drink plenty of water, eat Omega-3 foods
- Supplement Vitamins A and C, and Zinc
- A strategy to preserve eyesight, even if it has started to fail, is a combination of lutein and zeaxanthin, with Vitamin C, riboflavin, lycopene, selenium and turmeric.

Leaky gut syndrome

- Bone broth for collagen and amino acids
- Live cultured dairy (eg yoghurt, kefir) and fermented vegetables (eg sauerkraut, kimchi) to repopulate your biome
- Coconut products

- Sprouted seeds (eg chia, flax, hemp)
- Raw or steamed vegetables
- Fruits and berries
- Omega-3

Anti-inflammatory foods

- Leafy green vegetables such as chard and bok choy are good sources of Vitamins A, C and K.
- Celery contains Vitamins A, C and K as well as potassium. Interestingly it has no calories.
- Beetroot provides folate, manganese, potassium and magnesium
- Broccoli is a superfood on its own and provides a wide range of vitamins and trace elements
- Blueberries contain Vitamin C and K, and manganese, and are considered to slow cognitive decline, improve memory and general body functions.
- Salmon is one of the best sources of Omega-3, Vitamin B12, Vitamin D and selenium
- Walnuts are very high in Omega-3 and manganese.

OTHER USEFUL NATUROPATHIC PRODUCTS

Aloe vera: has antiseptic, anti-inflammatory, anti-viral and anti-fungal properties. It is used to soothe rashes and skin irritations, treat burns and cold sores, and as a skin moisturiser.

CoEnzyme Q10 is recommended for people with heart problems such as a history of heart attacks or coronary heart disease, high cholesterol (especially when taking statin drugs), high blood pressure, atherosclerosis or angina.

Further benefits claimed for CoQ10 include:

- helps lower fatigue and boosts stamina
- defends against free radicals and typical signs of ageing, including muscle loss and skin changes

- restores the power of antioxidants, including Vitamins C and E
- stabilises blood sugar
- supports healthy gums
- helps treat cognitive disorders, including Parkinson's disease and Alzheimer's.

Echinacea: a natural immune system booster used for countering infections such as colds and flu. It's also a traditional remedy for skin conditions.

Ginkgo biloba: traditionally used to improve cognitive function, reduce the risk of dementia, counter anxiety and depression, help maintain vision and eye health, relieve ADHD symptoms, improve libido, and fight fibromyalgia.

Ginseng: used to improve thinking, concentration, memory and physical endurance. It's also used to help with depression, anxiety and for chronic fatigue. It boosts the immune system, fights infections and helps men with erectile dysfunction. But beware, there are different types with different properties.

Magnesium: enhances cognitive function and joints, low levels correlate with allergies, hypertension and osteoporosis.

Milk thistle: promotes liver regeneration and is useful to counter the effects of excessive alcohol consumption. It can also aid the digestion and the skin and fight the appearance of ageing.

Saw palmetto: commonly used by men with prostate cancer, also contributes to a range of male health problems such as libido and enlarged prostate.

St. John's Wort (hypericum): used as an antidepressant, to relieve PMS symptoms, improve mood during menopause, fight inflammation, relieve skin irritation and improve symptoms of obsessive compulsive disorder.

There are many such products, and no doubt more will become available in due course.

Practical tips

- A variety of leafy green vegetables ideally should make up the majority of what you eat.
- Meat should be a 'side' dish and ideally be family farmed, grass-fed, and free range.
- 'Organic' foods are preferred because they shouldn't contain pesticide residues or preservatives, and should retain their natural bacterial load.
- Consider adopting the Mediterranean style diet coupled with a 5:2 restricted calorie fasting pattern (see links in Chapter 7).
- If you must gorge on treats, such as burgers or cakes, remember they have huge amounts of salt, sugar and fat, and keep it to 2-3 times a month. Or less.
- Some of the recommended foods are better raw or steamed since their active ingredients lose potency with cooking. An exception seems to be lycopene which is activated in cooked tomatoes.
- Cooking at high temperatures, high enough to turn things brown and crispy, can promote inflammation and in the extreme become carcinogenic. This includes crisps, fries, toast and roast meat. Smoked and cured meats come into the same category.
- Reduce grilling, frying, BBQing, roasting for the same reason as above (I'm sorry, I struggle with this one!).
- Use olive, coconut or rapeseed oils which are more stable at higher temperatures.
- Do more of stewing, slow cooking, stir frying, steaming, sautéing.
- Aim for variety in your meals.
- Use plenty of herbs and spices
  - add turmeric and black pepper to almost everything
  - use lots of lemon juice
  - be very sparing with added salt.
- Be alert to the tricks that supermarkets employ to make you buy more than you intend. Write a shopping list and stick to it.

- Read the labels on foods and put back those you don't like the sound of. Think of chemical additives as poisons to your biome. Get obsessive about this.

- Although red wine has been recommended in modest quantities, the most recent advice is that there is no 'safe' limit to alcoholic drinks. Try to keep it really low.

- It's hard to find some of the recommended foods and ingredients, so please be prepared to hunt. Favour local markets and farm shops with short supply chains. I've lived abroad a lot where there is less exposure to processed foods and where there is a more traditional horticulture-to-market supply chain dominated by smallholder production. I'm sure this is an advantage.

- Supplements are typically sold in specialist 'health food' shops, where they are packaged and labelled like pharmaceuticals. It can be hard to tell what is good, what quantities you need, and whether the price is reasonable. There's no easy short cut. It's best to do your own research.

- A lot of so-called naturopathic 'authorities' you can find online are trying to sell their own concoctions of supplements. But that's not necessarily a bad thing.

5 How to reboot your body

It's obvious that nutrition is important but, as we've noted earlier, health management is a holistic process that needs to embrace the whole you. There is plenty of evidence that:

- stress and anxiety can lead to serious physical as well as mental debilities
- disturbed sleep patterns can upset the gut biome and lead to weight gain as well as tiredness and cognitive problems
- a lack of exercise contributes to poor health and higher risks but relatively light exercise such as walking makes a big difference
- there are proven health and longevity benefits from frequent sex
- a sense of purpose, meaning and significance aids longevity
- a supportive network of friends, family or colleagues is a benefit
- curiosity and learning keeps the brain functioning and helps stave off dementia
- a pollution-free environment reduces your exposure to oxidation damage from free radicals
- your health is like your finances: the longer ahead you plan and invest, the better state you end up in.

In this chapter, we aim to provide some practical tips under all of these headings.

Managing your stress

Stress is caused by your body's response to real or perceived threats and challenges. Our bodies produce a hormone - cortisol - which helped us in our hunter-gatherer days to respond appropriately by fleeing, fighting or freezing. Nowadays, none of those are appropriate, so the hormone courses round our veins doing a lot of damage, especially if this is a frequent occurrence. Over time, the accumulation of damage causes inflammation and accelerates ageing. Stress may be as high a risk factor for heart disease as smoking and obesity.

Although you probably think of stress being caused by exposure to certain situations, or perhaps to certain people, it's the response in yourself that matters. That's what causes the damage but that's also where you can best tackle it. There is a long list of commonly identified stress triggers, no particular order:

- traffic
- queues
- finances, or lack of them
- personal relationships
- an unfulfilling job
- deadlines
- exams
- marriage and divorce
- bereavement
- worry
- giving a presentation or speech
- excessive workload
- high expectations
- danger or insecurity
- serious disease or disability
- unwanted commitments such as caring for an elderly relative
- traumatic events.

Stress can come from just thinking about such things, let alone being directly exposed to them.

Long term, or chronic, stress is dangerous to your health. It can cause problems in your gut, which you can feel, it can lead to psychological problems such as anger, anxiety, fear and depression, and it can be a cause of heart disease. Stress can seem to be ameliorated by feasting on sugary carbohydrates or alcohol but of course this just leads to something worse, that long list of ailments we've been trying to avoid all the way through this book. Managing stress, or learning how to cope with it, is a vital component in your health care strategy.

There is, by the way, an upside to stress. That fight or flight response can be turned to your advantage in the short term by using it consciously to face up to challenges. Most performing artists, for example, would agree that nerves are important in stimulating a great performance. The trick is to keep them under control.

There are four general approaches to controlling stress and minimising any negative feelings associated with it. All of them require that you first recognise and acknowledge your stress, and identify its likely cause.

Reduce, avoid or eliminate the causes

It may not always be possible or practical to do this, but it's clearly a good starting point. As with the other techniques below, you will need first to identify your stress triggers and consider what it is within the situation that creates your stress response. Is it something to do with the nature of the situation itself? Is it about another person? Could it even be about yourself? Then consider if it's possible simply to avoid getting into that situation or interacting with that person. If not, can you deliberately change your behaviour in response to the situation? For example, I used to feel noticeably stressed when stuck in traffic jams. Stressful situations often feature an inability to control them. So, using self-talk, which we'll discuss later, I reprogrammed my mind to use the time to think, to plan, or just to listen to some music. I was able to turn a stress response into a moment of relaxation.

Some of the most common and most difficult stressors are relationships within the family and at work. It may not be obvious that you can escape these but remember that long term chronic stress can kill you and it may be a perfectly valid solution to have the courage to walk away from a toxic relationship. It's often said that a stressful relationship with their immediate boss is the most common reason people move jobs. (By the way, if you're a 'boss', are you stressing the people around you?)

If you cannot separate yourself from the source of stress, there are two further options. I call them distraction and focus. Distraction means what it says: distract yourself from the source of stress by doing something else or thinking about something else. I know people stuck in difficult relationships who use dog-walking as an effective distraction. Focus means facing up to the source of stress and tackling it head on. This works best for situations like exams and speeches (and writing books!).

With many of these recommended approaches, I am only too aware that it is much easier to suggest them and to actually do it.

Relaxation techniques

One of the most effective techniques, which can be applied in many different situations, is deep breathing. Stress (or anxiety, fear or panic) tends to make us breathe faster and more shallowly. By forcing yourself to do the opposite - slow, deep and controlled breathing - you are effectively telling your brain there is nothing to worry about. Breathe in to a count of four, hold, and breathe out to a count of four, hold again. Repeat this ten times. You can do this in meetings, sitting in traffic jams, waiting for an interview, pretty much anywhere.

If your stressed state extends beyond the moment, you may also consider trying deeper forms of relaxation. These include listening to soothing music, taking a hot bath, yoga, meditation or enjoying the company of stress-free friends. Get onto YouTube and search for 'Alpha Music'. More about this too in the next chapter.

Mindfulness

Mindfulness has become a well known and often used technique that helps reduce stress through a form of focus: being fully aware of the present. It's a technique that involves simply paying attention to where we are, what we're doing and what's going on around us. In a sense, it's a form of meditation but one that can be fitted into a busy lifestyle anywhere, any time. You can download mindfulness apps which talk you through the process. They're very effective. Mindfulness has been shown to reduce stress and anxiety, cool temper and negative emotions, and sharpen concentration skills.

The technique I've found effective goes as follows. Sit somewhere quiet where you won't be interrupted. Close your eyes and take a few deep breaths. Focus on the breathing, slowly in and out a few times. Observe your thoughts, try to notice when they roam and bring them back again. Then pay attention to your toes, wiggle them, feel them. Your feet, flex them, move them. Keep the slow breathing going, keep observing your thoughts and catch them when they drift. Move your attention to your legs, your knees, how do they feel? Your thighs and hips, can you sense them too? Keep the breathing and your thoughts under control but don't worry if you can't, just keep noticing and trying. Move your attention to your abdomen and stomach. Feel them. Your lungs, ribs, chest. Your shoulders. Your neck. Move down your arms, feel them, flex them, sense them. Your wrists, hands, fingers. End up with your head, there is a lot to it, feel all the different parts. And go inside and smile at your thoughts and how hard they are to keep under control.

All that should take ten minutes, it doesn't matter, it's the process and the focus that counts. I'm not really sure why mindfulness works but after a few days of this you should feel the stress fall away. Your resilience should be strengthened. There are plenty of books and websites about mindfulness. It's a great practice.

Cognitive Behaviour Therapy (CBT)

CBT, which we shall return to in the next chapter, is based on the premise that there is a triangular relationship between thoughts, emotions (or 'feelings') and behaviours and that each can influence the others. Thus we feel hungry, which triggers the thought that we need food, which sends us to open the fridge door (behaviour). We think somebody dislikes us, so we feel upset, and we avoid seeing them. It can of course be positive! We listen to a piece of music (behaviour), which makes us feel energised, so we think we'll go dancing some time.

Equally important is to recognise what thoughts actually are. We tend to think we are our thoughts, or that our thoughts are some kind of deep reflection of the 'real me'. And that therefore, feelings emanating from them are also 'real' and therefore unchangeable. In reality, thoughts – and that dialogue that goes on in our heads all the time – are just the effect of chemical and electrical signals flashing between the neurons in our brains. Once you can 'see' this, then you gain the ability to observe and evaluate your own thoughts. And to change them if you want to, together with their influence on your feelings and behaviours.

In the context of stress management, CBT helps us bring to the conscious level both the triggers of stress and our responses to them. It's this business of making things conscious that enables us to tackle them. The advice is to use a 'thought diary'. When you feel stressed, make some notes in a journal. What are your feelings? How are they affecting you? What seemed to be the trigger? Reflect on your responses and consider what courses of action you might take from amongst those listed above.

Your own coping strategy

You need to devise your own coping strategy based on what works best for you. Some people feel they need professional help with this. But my advice would be to avoid the conventional medical-pharmaceutical route because it tackles symptoms rather than causes. In the long run, this means it doesn't work. But asking for help is a perfectly valid coping strategy in itself.

Getting enough sleep

Stress can lead to sleep problems and sleeplessness can cause stress. And it seems that a lot of people do not get their 7-8 hours of undisturbed sleep. This is a potentially serious health issue. Sleep disruption or deprivation increases blood glucose and affects the gut biome, thus promoting obesity and diabetes. Too little, and too much, sleep, over time, also appears to affect longevity. Sleep is essential. It's of higher priority in terms of bodily and mental function even than food and drink. Although scientists haven't yet figured out fully why this is so, sleep is when our cells regenerate and when the thoughts and memories of the day settle down into the appropriate places in the brain.

The conventional approach to sleeplessness is a pharmaceutical one: pills. This is a health risk in its own right and most sleeping pills are addictive and lose their efficacy with prolonged use. Alcohol and coffee both cause changes in the brain which disrupt sleep patterns. Mood, workload and your daily routines can all affect your sleep pattern. Natural remedies include herbal extracts such as valerian or the vapours of essential oils like sandalwood, frankincense, lavender or bergamot. The recommendations for improving your sleep 'hygiene' include the following dos and don'ts:

- don't try to sleep straight after a big meal
- make sure your bedroom is quiet and dark
- exercise regularly but not just before your sleep
- switch off all electronic devices
- develop sleep-time habits such as bathing or reading
- try using alpha wave background music
- root out sources of stress.

Exercise

Everyone seems to agree that regardless of how good your diet is, you also need exercise. There is less consensus on exactly what sort of exercise is appropriate but, in terms of a balanced lifestyle, reduced risk of disease and increased longevity, it doesn't need to be demanding. We're not talking about anything too arduous. Gyms, biking, or running have their place but that's not what I'm talking about here. What's required is at least 2-3 times a week getting out and walking. If you can do it daily, better still. The latest phone apps which suggest you need to do 10,000 steps a day are a bit over the top. But half or two-thirds of that is definitely good. An easy way to use your body at any age is to avoid taking the easy way: walk instead of drive, climb the stairs instead of using the lift, carry the shopping.

Aerobic activity is recommended to keep the heart in trim. This means pushing yourself hard enough to increase your heart rate and strain your breathing. Some people find jogging works for them, or cycling. Or see below. And to prevent muscular degeneration, some sort of resistance exercise is advised that actually strains the muscles a bit. This is particularly useful for the arm and shoulder muscles which otherwise don't get so well used. Stretching is recommended to help prevent the kind of muscular contraction that leads to stooping.

Sex

This is a valid form of aerobic exercise, so long as you put your heart into it! There is evidence that frequent orgasms (over 200 per year) correlate with longer life. Although most of the research is about men, there is no reason to believe it doesn't apply to women too. Again for men, there is every reason to think that the ability to have orgasms as you age shows that the prostate gland is still working. Talking of which, there seems to be little reason why people even in their 70s and 80s cannot have an active sex life. Done with love and passion, sex is both 'mindful' and good physical exercise, so it should be recommended more overtly.

Align your joints

My Arizona holistic health teacher took one look at me and said: "You don't stand straight". I was duly advised to consciously hold my shoulders back and stand taller, and get implants for my shoes. This was new to me. Look at the heels on your shoes. If they're worn to one side, then you too aren't standing straight. The danger is that over time your knees and hips will wear unevenly, the cartilage will become worn through, and bone-to-bone friction will damage your joints permanently. This can become one of the main causes of pain and immobility in later years. There are several retail outlets which will test the weight distribution on your feet and provide sole implants to straighten you up.

A pollution-free environment

The air quality in a number of cities is so bad that it directly causes tens of thousands of deaths every year. It seems to be predominantly caused by the exhausts gases of diesel powered motor vehicles, which is one reason that some authorities are actively exploring electric alternatives. In the UK, this has been partly due to a government decision to reduce tax on diesel vehicles due to their - at the time - lower fuel consumption.

This is a good example that shows why you should not trust your health to your government. For years there was a (successful) campaign to have lead removed from petrol, but instead we were left with the carcinogenic effects of diesel fumes and cities with over-polluted air.

Within the home and at work, exposure to man-made fibres, plastics and plasticisers, adhesives and other chemicals used in manufacturing furniture, fittings and buildings can trigger allergies and adverse reactions.

You might think that it's better to live in the countryside but that's only partly true. Even here you may be exposed to airborne pesticides and other chemicals used by farmers. As we've seen in earlier chapters, pollution exposure causes a mess of free radicals to swarm around your system, overloads your available anti-oxidants, and causes inflammation and related disease. Wherever possible, natural materials and a natural environment are to be preferred.

Breaking bad habits

If you really want to live longer, healthy and pain free, then it's quite likely you will need to change some of your eating habits, and perhaps some other things besides. I'm listing below some of the bad habits that are well known to contribute to physical and/or psychological disease. One of the best things you can do, for your own health as well as those around you, is avoid any of these you may currently be guilty of.

Smoking: this is the greatest free choice killer. You enjoy it? All your friends do it? It's 'cool'? You're still killing yourself. Smoking damages the DNA in your genes, which stops them fighting cancer cells. It also lines your lungs with a sticky substance not unlike tar, which makes breathing difficult. If you're a parent that smokes, you're encouraging your kids to follow in your footsteps, perhaps without realising it, dooming you all to a higher probability of disease and a shorter life. That's not cool. My friend Chris died earlier this month as I write from smoking-induced lung cancer. It was OK for him (no it wasn't), he was drugged to the eyeballs with morphine. But his wife and daughters were distraught. And it was totally avoidable.

Sugary carbs and fast foods: the number one cause of obesity and diabetes. They can be as addictive as the nicotine in tobacco. They can seem to relieve stress and uplift your mood in much the same way. But they will eventually kill you just as surely. Remember that most processed foods contain sugar and salt. They trick you by tasting good, but they're still slowly killing you. Fast foods to avoid include burgers and buns. I have to admit that more and more food outlets are offering what they call 'healthier options' but it's still necessary to check the additives in any dressings. The occasional pizza is not so bad.

Over-eating: too many people fill the voids in their day by snacking, and fill their plates with more than they need. One of the easiest 'new habits' is to simply reduce the volume of food you take in. Use smaller plates and avoid second helpings.

Binge drinking: alcohol is recognised as one of the main killers. It increases the risk of certain cancers and of liver disease. It can also be addictive. The recommended limit is no more than two small drinks per day. As for habits, it's better to restrict your drinking to two or three nights a week and not to over-indulge because that blows your entire weekly 'allowance' into the danger zone. Bingeing is a known cause of heart attacks and strokes.

Snapping at people: I'm constantly amazed (disturbed, actually) how many mothers snap at their children and wives at their husbands (and vice versa). I mean, is it fun? Do you enjoy being snapped at? Does it improve you to be constantly told off? Of course not. All it does is add stress on all sides.

Slouching: you can tell when people think they're old because they start to adopt 'old' behaviours. One of the most obvious is slouching as a precursor to stooping. Body and mind go together, so believe it or not, maintaining an upright posture can keep your mind alert too.

Exercise: taking up modest exercise such as walking and stretching is an easy way of reducing the risk associated with a lack of it.

Sunbathing: now here's a dilemma! We need Vitamin D which is made by the body in response to sunlight (and we lose it without sunlight). But exposure to the ultraviolet and infrared components of sunshine is dangerous to the skin. It can burn and it can disrupt the DNA in skin cells and cause cancerous conditions. Active sunbathing in pursuit of a tan is on the dangerous side.

Living with stress: stress can be oddly addictive. We can get used to it, and there is evidence that people continually fall back into stressful situations. But it is a long term killer and you need to find a way out.

Going to the doctor: especially in countries with free health services, people over-use and over-stretch the system, in case of the UK, to breaking point. The probability is that the vast majority of visits are unnecessary. Don't go unless you really have to. In any case, you most likely can't get an appointment until after your ailment has disappeared. Get into the habit of a) not getting sick in the first place, b) redefining in your mind what is 'sick', you can survive with a lot of minor ailments, and c) using 'health care' services when there is no other option.

Taking meds: talking of which, please get out of the habit of taking pharmaceuticals as a matter of course. In the long term, they are dangerous. Often they don't work, often they have side effects, and they don't tackle the real underlying issues.

Drink water: if you look carefully at older people, they often look shrivelled. That's because 70% of our bodies consists of water molecules. We can literally dry up. And that's a common cause of age-related frailty that leads to organ failure. The advice on adequate hydration is mixed, but it does seem that we need to get into the habit of drinking a lot more water than we're used to. A target of two litres / three pints a day seems reasonable, including tea, coffee and other drinks.

Planning your Third Third

The years up to our early twenties are all about learning and growing up. Our parents are, by and large, in charge. That's the first third: 1/3 = 25 years.

Then freedom beckons and for the next 30 years or so if all goes well, it's all about career, family, home building and money making. We like to think we're in charge, but in reality we're riding a wave that's carries us with its own momentum. As we pass 50, we know that's middle age. Kids fly the nest. Time starts to run out. We start to feel our age. That's the second third: 2/3 = 30 years.

As 60 approaches, we begin to think about what used to be called 'retirement'. We slow down, we forget things, aches and pains are more frequent, conversation turns to ailments and operations. The habits of the first and second thirds catch up with us. We're no longer defined by our family and career. Yet we might have 30 more years still to go. It's likely the longest phase of our lives, and, perhaps for the first time, we're free to make a lot of our own choices. This is the Third Third: 3/3 = 30 years.

If you're in this bracket and you're debilitated - physically or mentally or both - this phase can seen daunting. If you have older parents needing care, you'll know what I mean. It's demanding and it's not fun for anyone. But most of us seem content to cruise along at the mercy of age, family and the prospect of 'care', as if suffering is inevitable. It's not. You can plan how to navigate the third phase of your life with elegance and style. Using the advice contained in this book, you can stave off the effects of ageing, overcome discomfort and disease, and make your Third Third the best time of your life. After all, maybe for the first time, you're in charge.

> It's never too early to adopt healthy nutrition and healthy habits, and it's never really too late. But, if you have not already done so, you should aim to get serious in your 40s or 50s.

6 How to reboot your brain

Adopting new habits can be quite hard, but dropping old ones is the real challenge. I suspect a lot of people find that, in spite of their best intentions to change, they stay stuck with habitual patterns of both thought and behaviour. We're only really beginning to learn that this is nothing to do with 'weak personality' but, to a greater or lesser degree, a result of the way our brains work. And often a result of early childhood conditioning. How does this matter in the context of healthy living? All kinds of ways: putting up with long term situational stress; over-eating; comfort and convenience foods; excessive drinking; can't be bothered to exercise; addictions; anxiety; aggression, depression . . . it's a long list that directly affects both physical and mental health.

This is not the place for a deep psychological exposé. But I do want to share with you some relatively simple techniques for changing the way you think and changing some of the things you do (and eat). As with the advice contained in the rest of the book, these are based on people's practical experience (including mine) of what works. I've only included a brief summary of each but you can find out a lot more on the internet, The first step in all of them is to recognise the habit, or habits, you want to drop. Stop justifying it, or making excuses, and convince yourself of the benefit of change. Stop thinking "But that's just me, it's how I am". You can change. If you want evidence, pull out some photos from your childhood. Then look in the mirror. Is that the same person?

Just do it

When I decided to stop taking sugar, many years ago, I just stopped. I had to accept that tea and coffee would taste a bit different for a few days, and that sweet desserts would have to take a back seat, but that was it. There is nothing in the human body that requires sugar top-ups so this was a fairly easy decision. My wife stopped smoking one day in just the same way, fortunately before we met or our lives might have turned out rather differently.

One challenge of this approach is that some habits – eg smoking, alcohol consumption, gorging on processed sugary carbs – are chemically addictive, which is a good reason not to start them in the first place. Another issue is to do with lifestyle and peer pressure. The solution is easy to say and I know it's harder in practice: if they're damaging your health, then change your circle of friends and change your lifestyle.

A slightly more formalised approach is sometimes called the 3Rs: Reminder, Routine, Reward. Let's look at how this pattern works for giving up sugar:

1 - every time you make a cup of tea or coffee, remind yourself "I don't take sugar". Speak it out loud if necessary. Tell people.

2 - don't buy sugar, don't keep any in the cupboard, throw away any that's there now. The routine of tea making can continue in its absence.

3 - reward yourself with an indulgent muffin or cupcake (or whatever!) once in a while, while reminding yourself (and others) that you don't take sugar but it's OK to treat yourself from time to time.

You can work out your own pattern.

Self talk

That little voice in your head is one of the keys to success. It literally tells the brain what to think. You've heard all those tips about positive attitudes? The law of attraction? The power of visualisation? They work, if they work, by turning hopes into instructions which, so the theory goes, prompts you to adopt behaviour that supports the wish. You might have heard the voice talking apparently unprompted: "Oh go on, just one". Like other thoughts that take place in your head, you need to recognise it for what it is: just a firing off of neurons. It's not the real you. And you can prove this by consciously talking back to it.

I did this in 2017 to overcome a long standing nervousness about heights. I stood on the edge of the Grand Canyon's 3,000ft precipice by deciding I no longer had that fear and telling myself: "See, self talk actually works!"

Journalling

Talking to yourself works. But so does writing. It's often recommended to keep a journal about things you want to change because it gives you the chance to be a bit analytical and to come back after some time to see how things have changed. Journalling allows you to record facts (eg how many drinks did I have throughout June) but also feelings (eg how did I feel when I ate that plate of chips, satisfied or guilty?). You can keep a diet journal, a stress journal, a sleep journal, a 'dysfunctional thoughts diary' . . . it seems the very act of writing and recording jolts the brain out of its default setting and prompts different patterns of behaviour.

Neuro Linguistic Programming (NLP)

The three elements of NLP reflect the interrelationship between the way the mind works (Neuro), the words we use to talk to ourselves and to others (Linguistic) and our behaviours, or the things we do (Programming). The principles of NLP recognise that thought patterns can be identified and modified by, amongst other things, modelling the thoughts and behaviours of others. One of the NLP techniques I find helpful in the context of habit change is 'reframing'. This is a way of shifting your mental map. For example, while on my fasting days as part of my 5:2 diet, I reframe 'hunger' by telling myself (through self talk) that this is the feeling of losing weight. You can more easily live with it when it becomes a positive rather than negative feeling. You could reframe a craving for sweet foods, to give another example, by telling yourself it's your bad gut bacteria calling out in desperation. Or your need for nicotine by reminding yourself this is due to a chemical reprogramming of the brain, not an actual conscious desire.

As I write, someone is talking on the radio about people being discriminated against in jobs and in clothes shopping for being fat. They even object to the word 'obese'. This is an example of an effort to reframe 'obesity' (with all its negative health connotations) to a 'larger' or 'curvy' (but acceptable) body image. Unfortunately this also denies the responsibility for a well proven health risk factor by shifting it to employers and clothes manufacturers!

Mindfulness

We looked at Mindfulness in the previous chapter. Its value in helping to achieve change lies in the way it creates a powerful sense of 'in the moment' awareness. This ability to focus has been applied in all sorts of fields: golf, tennis, running, leadership, self-confidence, for example. There is no reason why you cannot adapt it to health and healthy habits. Be mindful of your body and what it tells you. Be mindful of your food and what it's doing to you. Be mindful of the relationship between your mind and your body. Numerous health benefits have been claimed for mindfulness:

- feeling less stress
- reduced likelihood of recurring stress
- greater ease of handling stressful situations and conditions
- generally improved cognitive function
- greater emotional control
- greater self awareness
- reduced anxiety and nervousness
- a permanent shift towards a more positive and less judgemental attitude and outlook.

CBT

As we saw in the previous chapter, CBT offers some interesting opportunities for helping to change habits, as well as its specific role in alleviating conditions such as stress, anxiety and depression. CBT is most commonly used to help people overcome more serious psychological complaints and behavioural addictions, but there is good reason to use its principles to tackle broader aspects of health where changes of habit are needed. For example:

- if you're struggling to stick to a new diet, use displacement activities to force your mind to think of something else
- if you can't keep away from sweet things, keep a diary of your feelings
- if you've persuaded yourself that, for example, being overweight, smoking or failing to exercise is somehow 'OK', CBT techniques will help you recognise and reframe those thought patterns.

Neuroplasticity

The brain's ability to learn and figure things out in different situations is a powerful evolutionary survival mechanism which enables us to adapt to different circumstances throughout our lifetimes. It suggests that change, and the ability to cope with it, has been a fundamental feature of human existence for thousands upon thousands of years. But only recently has the advent of functional magnetic resonance imaging (fMRI) enabled us to 'see' what goes on in the brain, and observe that mental adjustments ('learning') are accompanied by actual physical changes in the brain's neural networks. Changing its structure in response to habitual patterns of thought is referred to as 'plastic', that is to say 'mouldable'. Although most obvious in childhood, along with 'bodily plasticity', we retain this ability throughout our lives.

Neuroplasticity is influenced not only by thoughts but by our behaviour, emotions and the external environment. It is is the process by which all permanent learning takes place, such as playing a musical instrument or speaking a different language. It is what enables people to recover from strokes and injuries, overcome ADHD and other learning disabilities, pull out of depression and addictions, and reverse obsessive compulsive patterns. But it has its negative side. Compulsions and addictions are themselves due to a form of neuroplasticity. Environmental influences, such as exposure to certain chemicals in sensitive people, can trigger a kind of shut down in parts of the brain causing a form of 'stuck trauma' which, like depression, can lead to an inability to function fully in day to day life. Many people find themselves falling victim to similar if less serious 'stuck' phases in their lives when they find it difficult to break out of habitual patterns of thought and behaviour. Neuroplasticity explains how this happens, and also offers a possible way out.

There is a growing amount of evidence that the use of techniques such as CBT, meditation, and mindfulness, promote neuroplastic – ie permanent structural – change and enable people to overcome depression, anxiety or obsession and regain their mental acuity. It may sound odd, but we have the ability to literally tell the brain what to think and if we do this with determination and for long enough, new patterns can become 'hard-wired'.

Some of the principles that support brain rewiring are as follows.

- Change is mostly readily achieved when the brain is in the right mood for it. If you are motivated and ready for action, the brain more readily releases the chemicals necessary to enable change. If you're intensely focused on the task and really trying to master something for an important reason, the change experienced will be all the greater.

- The more something is practised, especially when you include a range of sensory inputs (eg visual as well as aural information, movement, colour, smell), the more neural connections are engaged.

- Initial changes are temporary and need to be reinforced. Our brains determine whether they should make the change permanent depending whether the experience is sufficiently rewarding or important in terms of behaviour.

- The brain can be changed by internal mental processes such as imagination, memory and visualisation in the same ways as and involving the same processes that influence changes achieved through interactions with the external world.

- Neuroplasticity is a two-way street - it is just as easy to generate negative changes as positive ones. We have a 'use it or lose it' brain. Entrenched habits that encourage brain change in the wrong direction are become more obvious as we get older and, because they are so deep seated, may take greater effort to reverse.

Music

Last night I was out watching a guitar duo play at one our local pubs. The glee in people's faces as they burst into a medley of old familiar Beatles tunes reminded me of the mood elevating effects of music and song (and dance). But I owe it to talented composer-musician Catherine Rannus that I've learned there is a scientific basis for this. In fact, that there is a form of therapy that has been developed around music using particular tones, frequencies and harmonies to tackle a range of conditions or or promote particular moods. According to Catherine's research, listening to music can aid relaxation and improve vital functions within the body which may be hindering overall well-being. Scientific studies have shown it can decrease muscle tension and blood pressure, and reduce anxiety. As we listen to music, our bodies release endorphins which are natural pain relievers. According to the tempo of the music, it may either stimulate attention and activity or produce a calming effect. The greatest positive effects appear to derive from live music.

Background music is used in public places, and by organisations and individuals, to manipulate arousal levels and moods. In hospitals, music has been shown to reduce pain, anxiety and stress, enhance the effects of anaesthetic or analgesic drugs, and speed up post-operative recovery times. Children, it seems, respond more positively than adults to all modes of musical influence. Listening to music on a regular basis can help children manage stress and anxiety while improving their concentration, focus and listening skills. Given the capacity of music to induce relaxation, it is not surprising that it is also able to induce and improve the quality of sleep. Neuroscientists have made a correlation between an increase of certain types of brain activity and the ability to reduce depressive symptoms and increase creative thinking. A number of producers have composed music to stimulate such brain waves and several have put up their compositions on the internet, especially on YouTube. I've provided some links at the end of the book. Tracks are available online or for download which can help with relaxation, stress relief, sleep, concentration and study.

Social networks

Older people often report feelings of loneliness and lack of purpose. Their sense of value, importance or significance in life seems to fall as children grow up and careers fade into history. This can give rise to negative emotions which may have a direct effect on health and longevity. It seems that strong social connections – family, friends, neighbours, colleagues – improve survival rates, by helping reduce negativity and stress and restoring a semblance of significance. There are more and more support groups available including 'meetups' or participating in activities or classes. There is some evidence that religion can also help to fill this kind of need.

Curiosity and learning

The saying 'you can't teach an old dog new tricks' alludes to our tendency to become set in our ways. But so far as the working of the brain is concerned, it's simply not true. In fact, there is evidence that learning new things keeps the brain functioning better and staves off the cognitive decline which is a prelude to dementia. There is another component to this which I haven't seen in the literature. With the world of work as it is, and more so as it is becoming, the idea of a single career with a single specialism is on the way out. The critical success factor now is the ability to learn new things and adapt to the changes that are going on all around us. We should be doing this throughout our lives. The concept of 'retirement' is going out of the window too, and people are more frequently working into their 70s and 80s. But my theory of the 'third third' suggests that the time you hit 60 is a great opportunity to do something completely different. After all, you have 30 years ahead of you. And, frankly, whatever you've been doing for the past 30 years is probably no longer relevant or fulfilling.

There are unlimited opportunities for learning, most costing little or nothing. Many are available online and if you are not net-savvy, that's something else you could learn!

Travel

Travel is valuable and therapeutic for a whole host of reasons. By taking you out of your customary environment, it gives you a new perspective on life which helps relieve stress caused by day to day routines and interactions. Travel is considered to be educational, and by immersing yourself in different communities and cultures, it promotes a greater understanding of other people and of our place in the greater scheme of things. Part of the explanation is that travel – and outdoor pursuits in general – help us to engage our hunter-gatherer instincts and reconnect with the earth. After all, we come from the earth and we return to it. Quite literally we are all part of it. Human beings occupied the planet by migrating around it. Migration – travel – is hard wired into our DNA.

While travel is valuable in all phases of life, a lot of people find that travel is something they can do more in their 'third third' when they have fewer shackles of family and employment. I'm afraid it's beyond the scope of this book to talk about how you might fund such activities but we should note that wise financial management is also a factor in your continuing health. Like your health itself, the earlier you start, the better.

You will probably realise by now that there are common threads in several of these 'mind changing' techniques, and that some of them are listed under 'body changing' too. The inter-relationship of mind and body is a rapidly emerging field of research.

7 Where to get help

In this final chapter, you will find some links, references and tips for making changes in your life that you feel are necessary. There are also some pointers for finding further information that lies beyond the immediate scope of this book.

It's tough to change, and it's tougher to do it alone. One of the reasons that programmes such as Weight Watchers and Alcoholics Anonymous work is that people participate in a group of fellow 'sufferers' under a supervisor. This provides an important measure of stimulus, encouragement and accountability which can make all the difference, especially as time goes by and the initial enthusiasm wanes. According to Patrick Holford, it takes 3 weeks to break a habit, 6 weeks to make a new one, and 36 weeks to 'hard wire' it. That adds up to the best part of a year, so don't underestimate the time and effort required. If you are trying to overturn a disease or debility, the rule of thumb is that it needs a month of focussed treatment for every year of prior suffering.

You may not easily be able to find a group, but it is very useful to find someone to act as a supportive coach or 'accountability partner'. It's a good idea if this is a person with similar goals to yourself. It's probably not such a good idea if it's a partner or spouse unless you have a highly supportive relationship. Failing these, you may be able to find professional support. Professionals exist under most of the headings we've mentioned earlier (nutrition, diet, mindfulness, CBT, NLP, etc). There are plenty of good resources online and especially on YouTube.

Your nutritional habits may be hard to change as much as anything because other people in the family may be involved. You need to recruit them to the cause. Healthy eating is for everyone, not just you alone, and getting children off to a good start helps them to hard-wire habits that should stick. But let's not forget we're talking about 'holistic' health and not just nutrition, vital though that is.

Health coaching

There is an emerging profession of people who call themselves 'Health Coaches'. It would better still if they prefixed with the word 'holistic'. Unfortunately, at least in the UK, practitioners are mostly either medically qualified but blinkered about non-pharmaceutical remedies, or specialised 'alternative' therapists offering yoga, aromatherapy, acupuncture, reflexology or reiki (for example). But if you can find one, I just want to remind you the long list of conditions that we believe you can avoid or reduce. Seeing them all in one place will help you understand why we call it a 'holistic' approach and how demanding this can be both for you and your advisor. Holistic health builds your resilience and promotes positive ageing, cognitive functions, organ function and your gut biome. The aim is to help you avoid or reverse a wide range of mind and body conditions including the following.

Mind: addictions, anxiety, chronic fatigue, cognitive decline, dementia, depression, over-eating, sleep problems, 'stuck' syndrome, stress, tiredness, toxic relationships.

Body: aching joints, arterial sclerosis, arthritis, brain shrinkage, cancers, colitis and diverticulitis, decreased mobility, diabetes, failing eyesight and hearing, heart disease, hypertension, macula degeneration, obesity, organ damage, osteoporosis, stroke.

Further information

There's a surprising dearth of information about holistic health, especially in the UK. These are some of the books and websites I've found useful and quoted from.

The 10 Secrets of Healthy Ageing, by Patrick Holford and Jerome Burns.

Health Defence, by Dr Paul Clayton, see website.

How Not to Die, by Dr Michael Greger, see website.

http://www.glycemicindex.com

- a searchable index of foods and their GIs.

http://www.montignac.com/

- Michel Montignac's original (1990s) exposé of the Glycemic Index and related diets.

https://thebloodsugardiet.com/

- avoid diabetes with a low carb Mediterranean style diet.

https://thefastdiet.co.uk/

- home page for the 5:2 fast diet.

 https://cleverguts.com/

- Michael Mosley's take on taking care of your gut biome.

https://www.patrickholford.com/

- Patrick Holford's website. See books above.

https://draxe.com/

- Dr Josh Axe's US site with lots of great information and advice.

http://www.drpaulclayton.com

- treasure trove of information and resources.

https://nutritionfacts.org

- Dr Gregor's plant-based diet website with a lot of useful video resources.

http://www.belightfulmusic.co.uk/

- Catherine Rannus' music therapy website

For information on Mindfulness, CBT, neuroplasticity and alpha wave music, just Google or search on YouTube, there are many useful websites.

Recommended supplements

There follow three charts showing the main supplements we need. They show likely typical intakes if you're on a healthy balanced diet (which maybe you're not), the published RDAs, a consensus optimum daily amount, and a recommended supplement quantity. The amounts shown are for normal health maintenance. Higher doses, sometimes a lot higher, and in combination, are recommended for reversing certain conditions. You may need professional advice in such circumstances, but it's not normally considered risky to overdose on these supplements.

Note: mg = milligrams, mcg = micrograms, please don't get them mixed up!

Vitamins	Typical	RDA	Daily need	Supplement
Vitamin A	1000mg	800mg	1800mg	2000mg
Vitamin B1	2mcg	1.4mcg	10mcg	8mcg
Vitamin B2	2mg	1.6mg	10mg	10mg
Niacin (B3)	40mg	18mg	60mg	20mg
Vitamin B6	2mcg	2mcg	10mcg	10mcg
Vitamin B12	7mcg	1mcg	15mcg	10mcg
Folic acid (B9)	250mcg	200mc	250mcg	200mcg
Vitamin C	60mg	60mg	550mg	500-1000mg
Vitamin D	3mcg	5mcg	15mcg	15mcg
Vitamin E	10mg	10mg	110mg	100-300mcg
Vitamin K	45mcg	-	95mcg	50mcg

Data source acknowledgement: Dr Paul Clayton, Dr Patrick Holford.

Minerals and trace metals	Typical intake	RDA	Daily need	Supplement amount
Selenium	35mcg	75mcg	185mcg	150mcg
Zinc	11mg	15mg	20mg	10mg
Calcium	900mg	800mg	980mg	100mg
Iron	13mg	14mg	10mg	-
Magnesium	300mg	300mg	400mg	100-200mg
Chromium	30mcg	125mcg	150mcg	120mcg
Copper	1.5mg	2.5mg	2.5mg	1mg
Manganese	5mg	5mg	8mg	2mg

Other additives	Typical intake	RDA	Daily need	Supplement amount
Beta-carotene	2mg	-	12mg	10mg
Lycopene	2.5mg	-	7.5mg	5mg
Lutein	1.5mg	-	7.5mg	6mg
Zeaxanthin		-		100mcg
Omega 3	150mg	-	750mg	600mg
Flavonoids	140mg	-	400mg	250mg
Isoflavones	5mg	-	45mg	40mg
Betaine		-		450mg
CoQ10		-		30mg
Glutathione		-		25mg
Pre-biotic fibre			8g	

A LonePenguin book
www.thelonepenguin.com
Strategic Alignment Ltd, York, England.

37700787R00048

Printed in Great Britain
by Amazon